BRANDS KEY

Brand	Owner
K-	James C. Shaw
Q	James C. Shaw
TC	Billy Bacon
⬥—	Guthrie & Oscamp Cattle Co.
7	A. H. "Heck" Reel
ꓕ	James C. Shaw
UH	Joseph Kennedy
C⋀	James C. Shaw
↶	Teschemacher & DeBillier Cattle Co.
ℏ	F. M. "Butcher" Phillips
VC	Senator George Cross
O—O	Sturgis & Lane Cattle Co.
14	W. F. Macfarlane
M	Kent & Bissell Cattle Co.
CR	Thomas J. Swan & Co.
45	James Reeder
♀	Hod Emerson - Emerson Brothers
Ċ	William C. Irvine
Ɪ	John Coad
⅄	Alexander Swan - Swan Brothers
∩	T. D. Jones
96	A. H. "Heck" Reel
⌒◡	Pine Ridge Indian Reservation
OLD	James C. Swan
t	William Guiterman
O7	Swan, Frank & Anthony Cattle Co.
◊	E. L. Baker
⌐5	James C. Shaw

NORTH FROM TEXAS

JAMES C. SHAW
From a daguerreotype taken about 1868 in Texas

NORTH FROM TEXAS

Incidents in the Early Life
of a Range Cowman
in Texas, Dakota, and Wyoming
1852–1883

JAMES C. SHAW

EDITED BY HERBERT O. BRAYER
ILLUSTRATED BY DAVID T. VERNON

Texas A&M University Press
College Station

First Texas A&M University Press edition, 1996
Manufactured in the United States of America
All rights reserved
03 02 01 00 99 98 97 96   5 4 3 2 1

Originally privately published in 1931 as *Pioneering in Texas and Wyoming:
Incidents in the Life of James C. Shaw;* second edition published in 1952
by Branding Iron Press, Evanston, Illinois

The paper used in this book meets the minimum requirements
of the American National Standard for permanence
of Paper for Printed Library Materials, Z39.48–1984.
Binding materials have been chosen for durability.

Library of Congress Cataloging-in-Publication Data

Shaw, James C. (James Clay), 1852–1943.
    North from Texas : incidents in the early life of a
range cowman in Texas, Dakota, and Wyoming,
    1852–1883 / by James C. Shaw ; edited by
    Herbert O. Brayer ; illustrated by David T. Vernon.
        p.   cm.
    Previously published: Evanston, Ill. : Branding
    Iron Press, 1952.
    ISBN 0-89096-730-x
    1. Shaw, James C. (James Clay), 1852–1943 2. Ranchers
—West (U.S.)—Biography.   3. Ranch life—West (U.S.)—
History—19th century.   4. Frontier and pioneer life—West
(U.S.)   5. West (U.S.)—Social life and customs.
I. Brayer, Herbert Oliver.   II. Title.
F596.S4   1996
978'.033'092—dc20   96-3103
    [B]   CIP

INTRODUCTION

IT WAS ONE of those hot, dusty, August afternoons when the grasshoppers seemed to rise in a cloud at every step and arc aimlessly away in short parabolas. The sparse gramma and bunch grass was already brown, and the old Wyoming cattleman bent down and pulled a tuff. Unconsciously he placed one blade between his brown-stained teeth. "Here," he held out several stems to me. "Too blamed dry. By this time it ought to be twice as high. This drought is one of the worst I can remember. When I first came to this country the wild hay was knee high in the bottoms, and along the plains the grass was dense and our cattle seemed to get more strength and weight from it than they do from the grasses we grow today." He brushed a brazen 'hopper off the brim of his grey Stetson. "This was the real cattle empire and we had "cattle kings" from one end of the range to the other. We raise better beef today, but the ranching business is entirely different from the range industry. I don't regret that part of the change, but with the old days went the greatest aggregation of cattlemen this country has ever known — "Tesche" Teschemacher, Fred de Billier, Will Guthrie, the Swans (Alex, "Black" Tom, and "Red" Tom), Moreton Frewen and his brother Dick, Francis Warren, Heck Reel, John Kendrick, Joe Carey, John Clay, Henry Sturgis, Fred Hesse, Billy Irvine, and many others. Yes, and as long as there is a western cattle industry the names of such Texans as Murdo McKenzie, Charles Goodnight, John Adair, Al Boyce and Dick Head will rank high as pioneers in this business of producing beef." We watched the devil-wind dissolve in the distant haze. As the old cattleman climbed back into the automobile, Walter Prescott Webb's significant summary of the cattle industry in America seemed etched across the sun-bathed expanse of burned grass,

> The East did a large business on a small scale;
> The West did a small business magnificently.

James Clay Shaw was neither a "cattle king" nor even a "cattle baron". He was, in fact, a typical representative of the ranching era which succeeded the breakup of the spectacular million dollar cattle companies and the disappearance of the "cattle kings" from the northern ranges. Following the winter debacle of 1886-1887, a majority of the larger companies were forced into liquidation, a movement further augmented by the disastrous Johnson County War and the paralyzing depression of 1893. Throughout the cow country small ranchers, many of them former cowboys and employees of the once dominate range companies, founded small ranching operations based upon acceptance —more or less grudgingly—of the relatively new elements in the old industry: fenced ranges and pastures, winter feeding, improved breeding, range conservation and water resources development.

Ranching became less colorful but more in tune with the changing character of the West. It was arduous work at best, but, for the men who worked to convert grass into meat, living and working amid the grandeur of the high plains country offered compensations not to be equalled in either the squalid industrial or the undesirable (to the cattlemen!) farm regions to the East. Despite recurrent droughts, harsh winters, flagging markets, and the continuous shrinkage of the area open to grazing, the cattleman and his family were wedded to the concept of unlimited time and space, freedom of movement, and individualistic action characteristic of the West. In many ways, and to many who lived there, it was more a concept than a reality, but it was one dream nearer to realization here than in any other place readily available to them.

Jim Shaw's fifteen hundred mile trek up the Northern or Texas Trail was commonplace among the youth of the Texas cattle country in the years from 1866 to 1886, but only a very few—among them his brother Tom and "Teddy Blue" Abbott—left so graphic a description of the highlights of such a journey. His arrival at Fort Laramie in the Autumn of 1879, after a visit to the Pine Ridge Indian Agency, marked the beginning of his sixty-three years of labor on the Wyoming ranges during their most turbulent and formative period. After a season on "Heck" Reel's HR ranch, he joined the Teschemacher and deBillier "Duck Bar" crew and for twelve out of the following thirteen years "ran the wagon" (as roundup foreman) for his wealthy eastern employers.

Jim was a fine roper and an excellent horseman even in later years when he became very heavy. He preferred a half-inch rawhide rope to the more common hemp and, with a typical cowboy's affection for fine horseflesh, selected and spent long hours training his own string of horses. (Like "Teddy Blue", who came up the trail from Texas the same year, he objected to his horses being called "ponies" and to his crew being termed "boys". "Hell, man, they were horses and men.") In later years he acquired fine Morgan horses, his roundup favorites being two seventeen-hands high named Marg and Missan.

When Teschemacher and deBillier folded up following their participation in the Johnson County War, Jim Shaw received from his grateful employers the old Duck Bar ranch house and headquarters buildings. To this he shortly added a homestead of one hundred and sixty acres and a desert claim of eighty acres. From the company's Laramie River ranch, where he had lived since bringing his bride from Missouri, he moved to the old ranch headquarters on the North Platte River. The necessity of raising grass as a crop instead of relying solely upon the free-will offerings of a capricious Nature, led to Shaw taking the lead in organizing the Bridger's Ferry Ditch Company and in doing a good part of the field surveying for that organization.

At the liquidation of the Duck Bar, Shaw bought in the bulk of the company's horse herd including most of the mares. Both Teschemacher and deBillier had been horse fanciers and their herd included a considerable number of fine Ethan Allen Morgan mares. Shaw raised the breed for saddle horses along with breeding draft animals from two strains of Belgian and Shire stock. It was a profitable business, but "by the time he was well established in the horse business, horses became practically worthless property."

Money during the 'nineties was difficult to get in Wyoming—as elsewhere. Jim Shaw had little of that commodity and took advantage of every opportunity "to make a dime." In addition to running his own ranch and rounding up and shipping for his neighbors, for several years he took the post of inspector for the Converse County and Wyoming Stock Growers Associations. As such he checked thousands of head of cattle brought in to Orin Junction on the newly completed railroad before they were permitted to start up the long dusty trail to Montana and the Dakotas.

In the meanwhile Shaw joined his brother-in-law, Bill Dodson, in the purchase and operation of a sizeable cattle ranch near the thriving mining camps at and near Silver City, New Mexico. In addition to buying large herds of yearling steers—many from Mexico but largely from Texas —Dodson went to Missouri and purchased a carload of fine Durham (Shorthorn) bulls. Despite a ready market for their beef in the mining and railroad construction camps in southern New Mexico, the Wyoming cattleman and his partner soon ran into trouble. Nine years of unrelenting drought finally had its effect on the ranges. The grass withered and died. Range water supplies virtually disappeared. Ranches on all sides were forced to suspend operations and many were completely liquidated.

About 1894 Shaw and Dodson began to ship their New Mexico herds to Wyoming. The move was timely. "Most of the big cow outfits had closed out along the Platte so there was range and fine grass everywhere." Shaw and Dodson bought all of the yearling steers they could afford in southeastern New Mexico for seven dollars a head, loaded them into railroad cars and shipped them to the old Duck Bar on the Platte. Buying out his partner in 'ninety-six, Shaw determined to concentrate on improving his own position. With the improvement of the cattle market around the turn of the century, and the liberal credit he secured in Omaha, Shaw increased his own production and began purchasing from four to six hundred steers every Spring. In 1903 he purchased a range in Billings County adjacent to the Little Missouri above Medora in North Dakota. He bought a herd in Texas and shipped it to Orin, where, along with fifty head of horses, he trailed them north to the new Dakota ranch. A second herd of a thousand native Wyoming two year olds was purchased from Olie Chambers and also trailed north. "That was a good outfit. Good men and good horses, but it didn't make much money. By 1907 it was about all closed out."

One way or another—for himself and for such other noted ranchers as Charles Coffee—Jim Shaw kept a round-up wagon running from 1881 to 1920. His ability and experience were valuable assets upon which his neighbors and friends frequently drew. Whether it was on the "Bacon Rind" ranch, the "Tug and a half", his own "Comical Q" or "T Cross X" ranch, he dominated both the work and the play.

Like so many other cattlemen in Wyoming during the first decades of the twentieth century, Jim Shaw earned a good living but not much more. His ditch company was not a notable financial success and though he acquired a con-

ix

siderable acreage, raised large herds and put up quantities of hay, his ranching did little more than produce the funds necessary for operations and for raising his large family.

Almost from his arrival in Wyoming, Jim Shaw took an active part in the affairs of the Wyoming Stock Growers Association. Though militantly independent and individualistic throughout his entire life, he was a firm believer in the efficacy of cooperative action within the cattle industry. He was assistant roundup foreman of district number five — which embraced the Duck Bar ranges — in 1882, and foreman for the roundups of 1884, 1885, 1886 and 1887. In subsequent years he served on the executive committee (1908-1914), was vice-president (1914-1917), president (1918-1919), trustee (1925-1930), and was elected to both honorary life membership (June 3, 1939), and honorary vice-president (1931-1943) of the association. When the ninety-one year old rancher died at his ranch near Douglas on October 28, 1943, the West lost not only an outstanding pioneer and progressive leader in the livestock industry, but one who, while appreciating the accomplishments of the past, continued to look forward to the future. At seventy-nine he had confidently written, "The best part of my life is yet to come."

Jim Shaw didn't set out to write an autobiography, but "to tell in a simple manner the story of my journey from Southern Texas to South Dakota." While this self-imposed limitation was regretable — for his life after 1885 was in many ways more interesting, if somewhat less colorful, than in the earlier period — the story goes far beyond the trail story he originally projected. In the archives of the Wyoming Stock Growers Association, deposited at the University of Wyoming, is the earlier draft of this story which he entitled, "The Texas Trail", and which is limited to his trail experiences. Expanded and including a graphic account of his early Duck Bar ranch experiences in Wyoming, the story was privately published in 1931 in a forty-three page limited edition pamphlet with the title *Pioneering in Texas and Wyoming,* and sub-titled "Incidents in the Life of James C. Shaw." Subsequently the story was reprinted serially in the Douglas (Wyo.) *Budget.* A similar account (in which some editorial corrections were made) was published by the Wyoming Stock Growers Association in its mimeographed monthly organ, *Cow Country,* and later serially reprinted by the eminent editor of the Cheyenne *Tribune,* John Charles Thompson, in his noted column "In Old Wyoming." Wyoming's distinguished author, Virginia Cole Trenholm, made excellent use of the Shaw story in her privately published, limited edition, regional history of "the La Ramie Region", *Footprints on the Frontier,* Douglas, Wyoming, 1945.

Jim Shaw's story is not just another cattle trail story; in fact there is little information on the actual day to day droving of a trail herd. Shaw was not the foreman or owner of the herd and was therefore not particularly involved in the management or economic phases of the drive. Curiously enough, the value of the story is enhanced by the fact that it is not a contemporary account written by a twenty-seven year old, largely inexperienced Texas cowboy, but the considered impressions (somewhat mellowed by time) of a mature cattleman, written at a time when he could select the most important (to him) incidents of his early life and place them in their proper setting. The result is an account worthy of permanent preservation. With the exception of some corrections in the spelling and capitalization of proper names, it is presented herein as originally written and as the third in the series of "vignettes" of the cattle industry prepared by the *Western Range Cattle Industry Study.*

Herbert O. Brayer

Evanston, Illinois

FOREWORD

THIS LITTLE book which I have attempted to write is the result of requests from nieces and nephews, who wanted to know some things about our family and incidents in my life when the West was young. So I have attempted the task, telling in a simple manner the story of my journey from Southern Texas to South Dakota fifty-two years ago. Many things are omitted, for the memory is faulty after a lapse of over half a century and that old trail ran through a country in which there was nothing to go by except rivers and an occasional army post.

My father, having a good farm, wanted me to be a cotton grower, but the idea did not appeal to me. I managed to attend a good school for two years at Elgin, Tex., and afterwards taught school for two years. I did not care for teaching, but I did want to see the unexplored West and so started out on the trail that led from the Gulf to the Rocky Mountains.

In those days it was necessary to travel with others, for the lone traveler was apt to lose his scalp to the Indians, or the Mexicans or other bad men who infested the country would rob him of all he had. There were many casualties on the trail and some are under the impression that the trail men were bad men. They were not, though, but conditions were hard and when a man had worked sixteen out of twenty-four hours, out all night in a stampede, horses giving out in mud knee deep, all kinds of weather, rain or snow, hot or cold, no wood, no fire, no breakfast—well, then when a man is so worked down he naturally isn't in the best of humor and quarrels come easy.

Great changes have taken place since I left my Texas home and came to Wyoming and it is a matter of much gratification to me that I was privileged to have a part in the building of a state from a wilderness.

The best part of my life is yet to come, but my recollection of events is so poor just now that they must await a later time to be written.

J. C. S.

Orin, Wyoming, March 30, 1931.

xiii

DAVE VERNON

North from Texas

I HAVE BEEN asked by my friends to write a short sketch of my life. On my part I will not try to make a "good story" or put on it any polish, but will try to tell as near as I can the facts as they have occurred to me.

My father, John Shaw, was born June 22, 1813, on the old Riggs farm on Cuivre River, in Lincoln County, Mo. My mother, Elizabeth Brow Norton, was born May 24, 1817, at a place called Somerset, Ky. My father's father was Irish. My mother's mother was Scotch and her father English. My mother's family moved from Kentucky to Missouri in 1831.

My mother and father were married December 24, 1835.
Nancy Shaw was born December 29, 1836.
Clarissa Shaw was born July 4, 1838.
William J. Shaw was born in 1840.
Sarah Evaline Shaw was born May 29, 1842.
Ninion Shaw was born July 4, 1844.
John Virgil Shaw was born June 30, 1846.
Mary Isabel Shaw was born October 17, 1848.
Abigail Frances Shaw was born October 17, 1850.
James C. Shaw was born March 17, 1852.
Jeremiah Wilson Shaw was born June 30, 1854.
Thomas Armstrong Shaw was born April 4, 1856.
Margaret Agnes Shaw was born April 4, 1858.

When my father started to settle he bought his land from the United States land office at Palmyra, Mo., and paid $1.25 an acre for it. The money for the land had to be in either gold or silver, and his talk reminds me that they had thieves in those days as we have now. I have heard him tell of the very strenuous times they had going over the route to the land office, how every mile of the road would be infested with road agents, as they were called in the West.

It seems as the wild game and fish got scarce my father got restless, and as they had heard many good stories about Texas he and his twin brother, Robert Shaw, got up a company, bought themselves some good horses and wagons and on the 1st day of May, 1852, pulled out for the Lone Star State. While they got through all right, they had a hard time crossing the rivers and guarding the camp, as there were some wild Indians and the tame ones in Indian Territory were none too good, as they would often steal the horses for a reward.

I must relate a story of my grandfather here. He had lived on an Indian reservation in Missouri until all the Indians knew him, and he was known to them as "Curly Jim." I have heard him tell how when the Indians broke out in the Blackhawk War the white people got together and made preparations to protect the settlers on the frontier. Curly Jim was made captain of a company of volunteers and while at first he had a rather good company, so many of the men had to go home for sickness or to aid their families that the company dwindled to about a dozen. The volunteers did all they could to protect the settlements. They caught an Indian chief and his men slipping back to kill a few whites and steal some horses. Both the whites and the Indians were hiding behind trees and logs to get a shot. The chief saw Curly Jim and called to him: "Is that you, Curly Jim?" Curly Jim said it was. "How many men, Curly Jim?" Jim said he had a hundred. "Whoopee," said the chief. "Too many for chief," and about thirty-five Indians were seen going over the hill. They got no horses or scalps of white people that time.

My father on his trip from Missouri to Texas had taken with him a good Morgan stallion and some good mares and had also bought cows. He did not do so well in the cow business, but did well with the horses. When the Civil War broke out he sold some horses as high as $300 and the cattle at high prices. He always traded the horses for cattle when he could. When the war ended he had a small gunny sack full of Confederate bills, not worth a cent. At the beginning of the war you could buy anything with this money, but as the war went on it got to be worth less and less and near the end of the war it was worth practically nothing.

The youngest three of the family were born in Texas. My brother, Jerry, was born in a tent under a large oak tree just as we settled on our land. We were strictly in the cattle business and when I got to be about 10 years of age I would be taken on the cow hunts, as they called them, to drive or lead the pack horses, which would be loaded with the bedding and grub for about five men. The coffee pot was a two-quart cup with a handle and was tied under the horse's neck. The bread consisted of biscuits, enough to last about three days, in a wallet, which was a sack with both ends sewed up and a slit in the middle to put the biscuits in. At times the pack horse would run away and kick the ends of the wallet off and the biscuits would fly through the air like clay pigeons. We would brand on the prairie and there would be good fun roping and tying the animals down. Each boy would have from three to five Spanish ponies, the grass would be always good and the ponies would be fat and buck us off. We seldom got hurt.

4

We often camped on Breshey Creek and our father would tell us to hobble the horses and take off our packs and he would catch fish for our dinner. We would build a fire and put on the coffee pot and in a short time he would come with the fish. We would leave the scales on them, roll them in the hot ashes for about 25 minutes and they would be the finest meat I ever ate. My father could always furnish us with plenty of fish, deer or wild turkey.

When the Civil War was ended the poor soldiers came home, barefooted, with little clothing and very much discouraged. They began to look after their farms and their cattle. They were very much discouraged and would brand anything that was not branded. During the war all the men were gone and while they were away there was no branding of the herds of cattle they had left. This put things in a bad way. The men who were too old or were crippled and were at home said not a word. Some of the old soldiers had contracted chronic diarrhea, which followed them to their graves. They were trained to fight and the ones who had been left at home had to take a back seat. I heard one old soldier say that it had made a believer out of him; that he ran away and went into the army, but after he had fought three years he would walk three miles around a blue coat hanging on a dead stump.

When the cattle would come on the creek for water I have seen as many as five head of mavericks in one bunch. These conditions did not last long after the old soldiers got home.

5

Before the war the small farmer did not raise cotton, cotton-raising being confined to those who owned slaves. The first year after the Civil War everybody raised cotton. We raised twenty bales, which averaged 500 pounds to the bale and brought 20 cents a pound, so we were rich for a while. The next year it went to 16 and 18 cents and it continued to go down until in a few years it dropped to 7 and 8 cents, and it cost about 10 cents to raise it.

Then the poor farmer's troubles commenced. In the spring he would not have a cent to start the crop with. He would go ahead until the cotton would begin to grow and show signs of a crop, then the merchant would allow him so much an acre on it, to be taken out in goods at the store, which would be mostly groceries. That part of the farmer's credit was abused until it was worth nothing, but it was the best thing that ever happened to the farmer. The speculators would have cotton buyers in every town along the railroads and every morning they would receive a telegram telling what should be paid for the different grades of cotton. In late years the farmer does not sell each bale as he gathers it. There is now a warehouse in town, where the cotton is stored until it is all in and the grower will have several hundred bales. The big firms bid on it and ship it out at their risk and in that way the grower gets the top price.

Most of Texas was a very healthy country until in the years along from 1865 to 1870. When everybody got to raising cotton and all kinds of melons along came malaria that brings chills and fever, the old fashioned ague, boils and sore eyes. In the summer and fall the quinine would cost about as much as the flour.

We had no time to go to school. With the cattle, the horses and the cotton crop, the school was left out. Texas has more money for the school per child than any other state, but the system at that time was very poor. In fact the people did not take kindly to the public school. All the schooling I received was after I was 23 years of age. I attended a grade school at Elgin, Tex., during 1876-77 and a part of 1878.

In 1873 the husband of my sister, Fanny, died and she asked me to go home with her and help her straighten out the business. Her husband's father, who was a man about 75 years of age, had taught school and preached all of his life, but he could out-cuss any man I ever heard. When we arrived he asked my sister if I was going to stay with her. She said that I had promised to help her straighten out the business. He then told her that he would boss the job, as he wanted his money. She asked him what money, and he told her that he had loaned her husband about $500 and now it would have to be paid. He had not been able to earn a dollar for three years. During that time he had been sick and she had nursed him and taken care of him just as though he had been an infant. She told him that she would be the boss and told me to go ahead as best I could. She asked him to show her some kind of a note and he could show nothing, but he said he would attach everything on the farm if she did not agree to pay him. She promised to pay him, but if he gave her any trouble she would take it to court and make him prove his claim. After that he was very quiet. I found three yoke of oxen, one mule team, a few head of cattle and some hogs on the range. I found the cotton in charge of the negroes, who were working the farm that year.

We hauled the cotton to the gin and settled up with the negroes. Then my sister had about twelve bales left and the old man told her that they would about pay the debt and she gave me instructions to turn it over to him. I told her there would be nothing left for her and the children to live on, but she said, "I want him satisfied and by the help of God and good will power we will get through."

I felt that we were doing the wrong thing to allow him to take everything there was in the way of a living from the little children, but my sister said that she was glad she could satisfy him and have him go to his people.

I had a hard time managing the negroes and running the farm, as I was young and not much of a farmer, but I have had as many old negro farmers come on the farm and advise me how to manage the negroes and the farm as I ever did white men.

In two years my sister got married again and I went back home. My sister said she was sure that at no time had her husband owed the old man as much as $500. During the summer after the crops are laid by there is about a month there is nothing to do on the farm. During the winter of 1873 there was a railroad built through the country from Bryan to Austin. When it built out to Rockdale it stopped there for about six months. This made Rockdale quite a town, as there was no other railroad for many miles. All north of Rockdale was a prairie country, with no timber except in the river bottoms, and not much there. There was a nice little town about eighty miles north called Belton, the county seat of Bell county. This Belton wanted all kinds of lumber and offered $1 a hundred for hauling it across the country. I thought that a good chance for a boy to make some good money and I got a negro who knew oxen to help me. I got four yoke hitched to a wagon, went to Rockdale and loaded every foot of lumber on the wagon that I could get on. The big wagon had been out in the sun all summer and it was dried out. The oxen were fresh and unruly and they started very fast, with the result that a hind wheel hit a stump and every felloe flew out of the wheel. Down came my load on the ground.

I cannot tell you anything about how I felt. The anticipation of driving the ox team across the prairie and the prospect of making $20 when I had not seen a dollar for months was the worst setback I ever got. When the lumberman saw what had happened he had an opportunity to look me over and had sized me up as a kid who had chosen a job too big for him. He came to me and tried to console me and advised me to give him back the bills of lading and he would give the lumber to some other team and after I had the wagon repaired he would give me another load. I came again in three days and the young fellow seemed glad to see me, gave me another load and a lot of good advice about the rivers and the road. I made three trips before I learned I was losing $10 a trip.

I was coming around a point and just at the bottom of the hill stood a wagon loaded with corn and one wheel off and a man standing by holding the wheel. My old oxen, being very contrary, pulled for the road and while I talked loud and strong to them it had no effect, though he and I hollered together. My hind wheel hit his hind wheel and jerked his wagon a few feet, but did no harm, but in his hurry to get the wheel on he let it run over his foot. He started for me. Just then I wished I was in my mother's arms again. He was a large man, with red hair and large dark freckles over his face. He had been shot in the face with a black powder pistol and one side of his face was black with powder. He was a bad looking man. He came loping at me, calling me every name any man ever was called and using more cuss words than I had ever heard. As he came I threw up my hands, telling him how sorry I was, but on he came. I had a hardwood whipstock in my hand, six feet long. I backed up a little and raised the whipstock to knock him down and he stopped still. I then used the best language I could find and told him how sorry I was. Then he calmed down and asked me to help him move his wagon out of the road. It was down hill and we rolled it out of the road and I ran on after my team.

When I got up to them I met three six-mule teams and my oxen had hooked the mules out of the road and were going on. The mules were loaded very heavy and did not want to give the road to an empty wagon. The first man I met with the mule teams said that if he could have gotten hold of my oxen he would have chopped the horns off of every one of them. He then told me where any man who would drive an ox team should be. The other two drivers looked daggers at me, but said nothing. I thought of home and mother and said not a word.

Sister Fanny had a hard time managing the negroes. One night a fox caught a hen and ran away with it. Sister called to me and I ran out and the fox dropped the hen. I brought the hen, which the fox had bitten in the back, to Sister, who put strychnine in the bite. There was a negro boy on the farm who would steal anything, but devoted most of his time to stealing chickens and eggs. He came over to the house that morning with his mother, who helped Sister with the household work, and Sister showed them where she had put strychnine in the hen and that when the hen laid an egg it would contain enough poison to kill two families and she was worried how she would take care of the old hen. But she chopped off the head of the hen and burned it. The negroes never heard of that part of the hen's career, but that boy never stole another egg.

When Sister got married I went home and my father was anxious for me to stay there. He gave me forty acres of the best land on the farm to cultivate, which I did. I worked very hard that year, thinking I would make some money and go to school for a year. The crop was not as good as I anticipated, and when I sold my cotton and paid my debts I had only $50 left. I decided I would not farm any more and about that time one of my cousins came from New Mexico and gave a good account of that country and said that good cowboys were making good wages there. About this time my brother, Virgil, had lost his wife and was very much depressed. He had two little children and decided to come in order that mother could help him take care of them. I decided to let him take my place on the farm. I sold him my crop of corn and oats and started to hunt another location.

A friend of mine named T. J. Bennett had gone to school at a private school at Roundrock, Tex., and said if I would go back with him that he could be a world of help to me, which he would be glad to donate. This I was anxious to do, but it was necessary for me to have some help.

I told this to my father, and went over as carefully as I could, telling him that if I could go to school about two years I would be able to help myself, then I could study medicine and some day be a doctor. My father looked at me earnestly and said: "Why, Jimmie, you would come back here wearing celluloid collars and cuffs and never be worth a cuss any more." My friend, Mr. Bennett, went to school at Roundrock one more year, then taught school two years, then studied medicine and made one of the finest doctors in Texas.

12

My father had a nice bunch of cattle a few years before this and as he was getting too old to handle them he asked my oldest brother, Virgil, to take them and run them on shares. They had talked it over seriously, but my brother did not want to run cattle. He said he would rather farm, that many of the men he would have to associate with had no good intentions and would rather steal cattle than play the game fair. He did not wish to go that route any more. I heard most of the conversation and I told him that Tom and I would run them. My father looked at me seriously and said: "Yes, you and Tommy would both be in the penitentiary within five years."

I have often thought that my father must have been a good judge of human nature. This was about 1871 or 1872 and everyone was driving cattle to Abilene, Kan., the end of the railroad, where they could sell their fat cattle.[1] My father let a firm by the name of Brymer & Townsend have his cattle and they never brought him back a cent. The Olive family lived just north of us and were good friends of ours, and good, reliable men, who would have taken our cattle and brought back the money, but my father picked the wrong men.

I was very anxious to go to school, but as I could get no help I decided to go to New Mexico. Cattle at this time were not worth much. Yearlings could be bought for from $2.50 to $3 per head, cows for $10 and 3 and 4-year-olds at $10, while at Abilene they brought from $15 to $18 a head.

There had been a man over from New Mexico that summer to visit with us who had told us all about how things were over there. He said that good, reliable cowboys got good wages there, but that the bad white men, Indians and Mexicans were busy along the way, stealing.[2] My brother, Tom, said if I was going to New Mexico he was going along. I was glad to have him go with me, but I did not think it was right for him to leave home, as he was then only about 17 years of age. I went to my parents and quietly gave them the information, but to my surprise they were not out of humor. They said they felt sure that Thomas was bound to go somewhere and were rather glad to have him go with me.

About December 15, 1875, we got together two good saddle horses and a good pack horse and started for Santa Fe, N. M. I think the distance was about 500 miles. We had our grub and bed packs on the horse and did not expect to stay at houses. The first night it rained and we got wet. The next morning we went through Austin, Tex., and there we armed ourselves with all kinds of guns and plenty of ammunition. That afternoon it rained and we got wet again and a norther came up and we stopped at a house in a small town called Oatmanville. We went on next morning, but did not feel well. We were on the Fredericksburg road, leading to Santa Fe. When we came to the road running to San Antonio, Tom said if we wanted to go to a place where there was plenty of money we had better go to San Antonio, that people had told him you could see the gold stacked up against the windows as you passed along the streets. I said, "No, we are going to New Mexico."

We camped out that night and in the morning we were both sick. We made coffee and drank it, but could not eat a bite. We moved along that day and got to the Blanco river that night, crossed over and, as it was raining, we stopped at a nice looking house. Next morning we could not get out of bed. An elderly man came in next morning and asked if we knew or had any idea of what was the matter with us, if we had the measles or if we had any chance to take the smallpox. This man seemed to be about 50 years of age, but had a young wife and two children. The children would amuse us all day, when we should have been asleep.

We could not eat anything, but the lady would try to induce us to and did everything for our comfort, but it was in vain. On about the third day the elderly gentleman said that we had better have a doctor. This did not sound good to me, for we were not favored by plenty of cash and I could not see how we could give up one of our horses. I told him that I thought that I was better and could not at that time see how I could have a doctor. He said he was going to Blanco City that day and would consult a doctor and bring back some medicine. When he came in that night he brought in the medicine and doctored us as he thought best. By this time Tom could not walk, but the man did all he could for us, using the medicine and anything he had on hand.

Anyway, in twenty-four hours we felt better and the first day that Tom could walk it was nice and sunshiny. I got him to go down to the river and I knew by his looks that he was at least on the mend. I found out that he had slept very sound the night before from an incident that happened. There was a one-legged negro on the place who slept in the room next to ours. The old man would call him in the morning to build the fire, and there was always but one call. This morning the poor boy let sleep get the better of him and the old man came out with a cane, got poor Negro Tom by the leg and went to work on him. Of all the yells I heard in my life, poor Negro Tom made them. I remember a few things he said: "Oh, Mastah, you are killing me. Oh, my God, soften dese licks and I'll nevah forget you. Oh, my God, soften old mastah's temper," and a few other things like that. I am sure the yells could have been heard for miles. Next morning Negro Tom rolled a barrel on a wheelbarrow to the river to get water while Tom and I sat on a large white rock on the river bank. I said I wondered how the negro's back was by now. Tom looked at the negro and asked what was the matter with his back. I asked him if he had heard the old man call him this morning, but Tom had never heard a word.

I said to Tom that our horses were now in good shape, as the old man had fed them grain all the time, and that our bills would be large and we might have enough money to pay them, but I doubted it very much. Tom got up and looked down the road and said: "If ever I start out again it will be that way," pointing towards home. I wanted to be brave, but it took all the will power I had to say that I thought we had better continue on our journey. Tom said no, and just then I wanted to hug and kiss him, as I was never so proud of a boy in my life.

We sat there by the side of the road from Fredericksburg to Austin, where there was a large passenger traffic and where the trade demanded two large six-horse stage coaches each way per day, and on the bank of the pretty river, and we talked it over pro and con, but Tom insisted that just then to see mother beat any gain or bit of fun that we had ever had. I was with him, but I had to talk the road to the west.

The little woman had done everything for us that was possible for anybody to do and it seemed that she was willing to do more. Tom thought that if we were starting for home next morning he could ride, so that night I went in to talk to the old man about conditions and how it would be on the trail to Santa Fe and this is the advice he gave me:

"If I were you I would go back home. It is three or four hundred miles across and I doubt very much if you boys could make it. The Indians are bad over there and there are roving bands of Mexicans who will rob you and steal your horses.[3] The white men as a usual thing are not good men and it being winter I would not try it."

The next morning the old man and Negro Tom brought out our horses and we packed up. It took both of us to get Tom on. Before we started we pulled out our money and handed him what we had, which amounted to about $32. He looked it over and asked us how far we lived. I told him about a hundred miles. He said: "You will still owe me this much, but I will give you back $5."

We loaded Tom on his horse and started down the road. Tom had a fine horse and a good roadster that could take his gait at a fox trot and make six miles an hour and do it easy, but he could only ride about five miles or less and then get off and rest. Then I would have to help him on again. The good woman had put us up a nice lunch and it was a nice, warm day. We made coffee and ate our lunch, but it rained that afternoon and we stayed at a house that night in a place called Dripping Springs. Tom suffered, as he was very tired, and the young people at the place seemed to be having a dance or some other lively doings. As soon as we had supper they sent us to our room. Tom tried to sleep, but there was no sleep and finally Tom said he wished the fiddler would die before he could start another tune.

Tom was better the next morning and we got an early start. We got along good that day and got home the next night in a driving rain. My mother ran out to meet us and was glad to see us. I said: "Mother, you're not expecting us?" "Oh, yes," she said, "I knew that you would soon return to your father's roof." I took exceptions to this and said: "Mother, the next time I go I will not return."

Home did not look good. My youngest sister, who was the life of the family, had married, and my brother, Jerry, had married and it just seemed there was no home. The next morning I started out to get work. I went to see a man by the name of John M. Whipple, who wanted a man. I told him I was a real farm hand and wanted a job. He looked me over carefully and introduced me to Mrs. Whipple and asked if she thought I would do. Mrs. Whipple was very nice and said she thought I would be satisfactory. Mr. Whipple then asked me if I could milk cows, feed horses, chop wood and plow. Whipple was raised and educated in Chicago, had taught school and preached all his life, but was a stranger to a farm. He had married a widow with a nice farm. He told me he was paying negroes $12 a month and that they made good farm hands and that was all he would pay me. I went to work. I could see that Whipple liked to have a big, black negro called Alfred and one day when I was having trouble he called Alfred to drive my team. I told him to give me my money and Alfred could drive both teams. He said nothing, but went into the house as if in a hurry. I was there about ten months and I got about $30 when I left the farm and an order on a store for clothes. I got a suit of clothes, shoes and boots on the order and that was all I got. I gave my brother-in-law, McDonald, who ran a livery barn in Elgin, an order for a load of corn and he got that. However, I learned two new words. I went to see Whipple when he promised to pay me and when he saw me coming he stuck his head out of the door and said:

"James, that little matter between us will have to stand status quo." I learned that that meant there would be no change.

My sister, Sallie McDonald, traded the little farm my father gave her for a hotel in Elgin and was doing a good business. She asked me to come and stay with her and go to school. I made up my mind that this was the best opportunity I would ever have to go to school and in November, 1876, I started in. Old Professor Isaac Stevens was in charge and I had been to him before. He wanted to do the best he could for me, but had a hard time getting me fixed up. He lined out a course of study for me and helped me all he could. Some of my classes were with boys 12 years old, while some were with grown men. The school was out in May and I hurried out to see what I could do. I was out of everything, but some good friends of mine got me a summer school.

This little school was made up by subscriptions at the rate of $1.50 a month. I had boys there 21 years old, a lot of 18 and 20 years, while there were some very small ones, 6 to 7. The school was in a good location in the country and we opened it about the second Monday in June, 1877. There were some big girls, about 15 or 16 years of age, who thought themselves about grown. I opened by telling them that this was a short term and that I would have no set rules or by-laws for them to go by nor no serious punishment for them. All I wanted was good behavior, good manners and a desire to learn. All I could promise them was that I would do the best I could for them.

I had about thirty pupils and they were all industrious and enjoyed their work. It made me glad when the boys in after years came and told me they learned more there in the same length of time than they ever did any place else.

I returned to Elgin in September, 1877, and went to school with the same old bunch and the same teachers. My mind by this time was a little better trained and it was not so hard for me to keep up with the class. I realized that this was a golden opportunity for me and I did my very best. One little thing happened that is worth repeating. In the town of Elgin lived a man by the name of Joe Bennett, an old bachelor who ran a keg saloon and ran it himself. He was a good friend to Mr. and Mrs. McDonald and to me. Mr. Bennett got sick and McDonald had to run the saloon for him. Bennett slept in a back room of the place and was not satisfied unless someone slept there. McDonald, because of his work with his livery barn, could not do it and that left me to sleep in the saloon.

McDonald would run the business all day and when closing time came at 10 o'clock I had to be there. In those days I never thought of taking a drink and did not like to associate with those who did. I hated saloons and never went around them, and to sleep there seemed to me nothing short of a crime. It seemed as if Bennett never would get well.

21

I never finished my school work until 11 o'clock and I got up at 6 o'clock. As soon as I got in I locked the door, but there would be somebody rattling the front door until 12 and that door would start rattling again at 4 in the morning.

A keg saloon is where the customer comes in and turns the faucet in any keg he wishes, takes his drink, lays down his money and goes out, so that I did not have to handle either the money or the whiskey. It almost caused me to lose out in my school work and the ten days I spent there were the longest I ever knew.

School ended on the 26th of May and I was almost finished with it. T. J. Bennett had taught school the year before in the Conly school in Milam County and there were a number of boys and girls over the lawful age who were to pay $1.50 a month, but when the school ended not a dollar could be collected. The people were willing to settle their obligations, but they had no money. The school was out in the spring, but cotton was not marketable until fall. Bennett made them all give him notes for the amounts owed. He gave me the notes and said he would give me a good per cent or he would loan me the money without interest until I could commence to earn some for myself. As soon as school was out I went to the Conly community to collect, as I did not have a cent to my name. Bennett loaned me a horse in remembrance of what I had done for him in the saloon business. All of the people had cattle and I took these for what was owning, paying $5 for yearlings, $7.50 for 2-year-olds and $10 for cows and 3-year-old steers. I had no trouble in collecting all of the notes in two days and was on the road with a small bunch of cattle.

Just then Al Boyce was getting up the last herd for Snyder Brothers at Georgetown to go to Iliff, on the South Platte, in Colorado.[4] I was sure I could sell the cattle to Boyce, but on going up Breshey creek I got to Cal Barker's ranch and after dickering a long time sold them to Leamon and Nat Barker for just what they cost me.

Just about this time things were not looking good in our country, and I was anxious to get a location where I could earn some money in a legitimate way. A friend of mine that I had been with in school started out for Comanche County, Texas, to visit with our old friend, T. J. Bennett. We arrived at Bennett's home on about the 10th of June, but he had taken a summer school in Jonesburg, about 60 miles from his home. After my friend, Dov Mc-David, had hunted and fished for a few days, he returned home and I went down to see Bennett and brought him to his home.

Bennett had a drug store at Jonesburg and was anxious for me to take charge of it, but I told him I would not tie myself down until I learned the drug business. He insisted, saying that the man in charge, who was going away to study medicine, would stay until he taught me. Still I refused the offer. Then he wrote me a good recommendation to the school board of the county school and when I went to see

23

them in person they gave me the school. Then came my first trial to go before the examining board to qualify as a teacher. At that time the schools in Texas were in bad shape. There seemed to be plenty of money, but organization was lacking. The people of the South did not take kindly to the public free school and it was many years after the Civil War before a real public school system was organized.

I had to go before the district judge and county clerk and when the judge was absent it was his clerk who acted. He began the examination with English history and he did not go far until he found that I was not posted. Then he got down to the things we were supposed to teach in our country schools and he complimented me and said that I was very good and gave me a certificate.

When I had about finished a Negro came in with a petition signed by all the Negroes in a community for a teacher. The judge told the clerk to start in on him. The Negro was a fine physical specimen, but had no training whatever to fit him for the place he was seeking. The first question the clerk asked was "How are you on grammar?" He looked as surprised as one could and said: "Gramma? What is that? I nevah heard of that befo today. Dey shore nevah had that in the school where I went."

"Can you read?"

"Yes, sah, some."

"Can you write?"

"Yes, sah, a little."

"Take this pen and write a sentence."

24

"Now, sah, how you hold this pen?"

The clerk fixed the pen in his hand.

"Now, sah, what I write?"

"Just write Austin is the Capital of Texas."

"Now, sah, what letter do dat begin with?"

"It begins with an A."

"Oh, yes, sah. Now show me how you begin to make that A."

Then the clerk showed him how to make the A and the judge told the clerk that those colored people wanted this man to teach them and would have no other and to give him a permit for three months. This was at Cameron, the county seat of Milam County, September, 1878.

On the 1st of October, 1878, I opened school at the Conly school house in Milam county, Texas.

On the first Sunday after I opened the school I had the pleasure of hearing Rev. Conly, the man after whom the school and church were named, preach an impressive sermon. Mr. Conly was then 75 years of age and feeble. He was very tall, with a long white beard and a kindly face. His text was: "A man is like a blade of grass that groweth up and flourishes in the morning, but withereth and dieth in the evening." I always had the greatest respect for Mr. Conly after that.

I boarded with an old lady who had a son about my age. Her name was Stiles. I paid $10 a month for my board and $2 a month for my horse. I had about forty pupils, including some grown-up boys and girls. Captain John Moore, father of Lee Moore, well known Wyoming pioneer, was one of the directors of the school and was always willing to help.[5] Some of his children were in the school. Mr. Snively was another director and made many visits to the school. A noticeable thing about him was that he always carried a first class double bore shotgun with him.

My school ended about the 1st of March and I then went home. My brother-in-law, Israel Duey, had another one laid out for me, at the Sam Smith Springs schoolhouse. I started there in March with 25 pupils, but this was for only the latter part of the term, which ended on the 5th of May. On the 10th of May I started north.

In the spring of 1878 my brother, Tom, started north and at Austin met Hi Webb, who wanted men and who was then on his way to San Antonio to buy horses. From San Antonio they went south to the Gulf of Mexico and secured a herd.[6] They started north with the herd, swimming all the rivers from the Guadaloupe in South Texas to the South Platte. When the herd was sold at Ogallala they went to Cheyenne and Tom hired out to Arthur Coffee to go to Green River to bring a herd into Wyoming that was coming from Oregon.[7] This herd was sold to Howard and Will Warner.[8] John Rees was running the outfit and asked them to deliver Tom with the herd, which they did, and Tom had a job. Tom then wrote me about the trail work and the country and I was anxious to try it.

I HAD TWO horses of my own and Tom had left me two. I traded one of my horses for a saddle and a six-shooter and started out with a pack outfit to catch up with a herd that would be at Fort Griffin about the 23rd of May.[9] That spring there was a lot of people having flux, which ordinarily was not a serious disease, but this year about a fifth of those taken down with it died. I had seen one or two die with it, and I was afraid of it. About the third day out I was taken with the flux and took some medicine for it, but it did me no good. The fifth day I landed at old Father James Bennett's home, where I knew I was welcome to stay until I got well. Mr. Bennett was a fairly good doctor. I stayed there five days, until I was well again. The boys had taken good care of my horses and I started out again.

On the fourth day I landed at Fort Griffin, on the Texas frontier. There was a good post there, with about 400 soldiers and a small town. The soldiers were camped five miles up the river. The night before I got to the post I stayed at a cow ranch. They were corralling about 500 steers as I came up and the men told me to hobble out my horse and stay all night, which I was only too glad to do, as I had had nothing to do that day. We had supper and after everything had been cleaned up one of the men spread a blanket on the dirt floor, hauled out a deck of cards and told us to get in. There were two men and a boy about 18. One of the men was a man about 40, very dark, with a long black mustache, the other man was not so old, tall, sunburned, with a large mustache. Each of the men had six-shooters, but had hung them on the wall when they came into supper. I told the fellow that I could not play cards and he did not insist, but told the boy to sit in. The boy proceeded to get out his money, as did the others. The boy had about $40, but in an hour he didn't have a cent. Then he wanted to quit, but the others said the game must go on. The boy insisted that he had no more money, was tired and must go to bed. The men said he had two good horses and a saddle and with that talk the boy sat in again. One of the men put up his horse against the boy's horse and finally won both of them. The boy then wanted to quit, but they told him he still had a good saddle and they would put up $25 against it and give the boy the deal. The boy brought in a good saddle and I began to feel sorry for him and said: "Oh, boys, don't take his saddle away from him." The dark fellow gave me a wicked look and said: "You better attend to your own business and let mine alone."

I slipped out and went to bed. The next morning the boy told me he had been out there a year and had got some money and two good horses and was going to Fort Worth with those steers and then go home. He said his mother had a little farm and was getting along poorly and he had written her that he would soon be at home with some money and two good horses. Then he said: "I can't go home now. I think I will borrow some kind of an old saddle and a horse and go to work again."

At the Fort there was a string of men going into the saloon and one tawny young man came out and asked if I wanted work. I told him that I had expected to catch up with a herd there, but was about a day late and was busted. He said: "Come and work for me. I will give you $25 a month to make hay on Sweetwater." I told him I would see about it. As no one stopped outside I went into the saloon. Several asked me to have a drink, but I declined, saying that I could not drink. After things cooled down and there was no one around, the man on the job, who was about 50 years old, one-eyed and very thin, said: "You don't drink, I see." I said, "No, I never drink or smoke." "That is right," he said, "neither do I." Then he said: "You seem to be a stranger here." I then told him my story. "Why don't you go on and catch up with the herd? They crossed the river only yesterday." I said the river looked bad. "I saw you talking to Lou Millet, did he want to hire you?" I told him he did, that he had a hay contract on Sweetwater and wanted me to help. "Now, as you seem to be a stranger, just like I was once, I will give you a little advice. Several years ago I came to Abilene, Kan., and was busted, with no friends. I fell in with just such an outfit as Lou Millet has up there. They would all go to town, come back drunk and shoot up the camp. They would gamble all night and the more decent ones never had a dollar. I got tired of it and another fellow and I started out to kill buffalo for the hides. We were getting along good until one day one of those bad men came along and wanted to throw in with us. He had money and some horses and we let him in, but he would never lay off that six-shooter, but would play with it from morning until night, turning it on one finger and cocking it as it went over. One day he let it go off and shot out my eye, and I have had no use for those six-shooter men since. Last week there was one of them standing in the door of the hotel, turning the pistol the same way. An army officer came out and told him there were women and children in the hotel who would not like to see that, but the fellow never stopped. He said that a little six-shooter bullet would not hurt anyone. The next day he was doing the same thing when the gun went off. The bullet went down his side and he hollered so loud that everybody in town heard him. Millet and Maybery are running a large herd of cattle up Sweetwater and Lou Millet has a contract to furnish the post with its winter hay, but he wants you to skin buffalo and fight Indians. He has a lot of bad men who get the easy jobs. The men you see around here are one and two-time men killers and I would not go about with them. You can swim the river and catch the herd tonight, and I would do that."

I had just 50 cents and I bought a biscuit or two and a small piece of bacon and made for the river. I got across, soaked, and everything in the pack was soaked. This was one of the important rivers of Texas, the Brazos. This was the twenty-fifth of May, 1879. I was now in Throckmorton county and there was nothing in sight. There were no settlements from there to Indian Territory, 150 miles away, and many wild Indians. I poured the water out of my boots while the horses grazed and then took the trail where the herd had gone. This was a fine range country and this was about the only herd that had gone across there. As these cattle had been driven from the coast in a hurry to catch up with the other herd at Fort Griffin, so the two could be thrown together, they were very tired and the foreman had orders to graze them for a few days. There were then 1,500 big steers, 1,500 cows and 1,850 steer yearlings. This was the sixth herd that Ellison and Sherrill had put on the trail for Ogallala that year.[10]

The cattle scattered out, so they did not make a very distinct trail and I lost it, being so busy looking out for Indians. I stopped on the bank of a pretty little creek where the grass and water were good and where there was a large grove of elm trees. I broiled my bacon on a stick, but my bread and coffee got soaked while I was crossing the river and were not fit to eat. When it grew dark I hobbled two of my horses and tied the other to a mesquite tree at my head, giving him plenty of rope to graze. I lay down to sleep with a gun in my hand. I was pretty much a tenderfoot these days. When I left home both of my parents begged me to stay and my mother came out to see me go. I could hear her crying until I was out of sight and that worked on my feelings. That night in my dreams she came to me as she had done of yore and asked if I was warm and comfortable. About 2 in the morning it began to rain and I got up and sat against a mesquite tree. I had gone to sleep again when lightning struck one of those elms. I reared back just as the horse jerked the small tree, which took all the hide off the back of my head. It rained hard then, with a north wind blowing, and I could hear the cattle bawling a few miles north. I think that was the most dismal night I ever spent and how glad I would have been to have been with my parents, well and happy.

I started out at daylight and just down the valley an Indian came down the hill and started to head me off. I thought at first I would try to outrun him, but as it got lighter I could see that he was wearing a hat and riding a very tired horse. I stopped and he turned toward me and I toward him. He said: "How, and where did you stay last night?" He was not an Indian, but one of the men from the herd. He had gone back to Fort Griffin and had lost the trail, as I had. He had sat on the hill just above me all night. He said I should have heard him shoot when an antelope had run up to him and scared him, so he shot at it. We talked about where the herd was and I told him of hearing the cattle bawling in the night. He said that certainly was the herd and for me to go ahead in the direction I heard the cattle bawling. His horse had given out and I offered him one of mine, but he said he would ride his own a little farther. We came to another creek in a few miles and there we found another outfit. They had had their cattle in a corral and the storm had caused them to break out and they were the ones I heard. This creek was out of its banks and had washed a lot of fish out and the men were having a fish breakfast. They asked us to eat, which we were glad to do. Just then a man of the party came up and said the herd was just up the creek, trying to cross, and was having a hard time of it. Then he got one of my horses and I trailed one of mine to his horse and led his. When we got up to the herd all of the cattle had crossed except about a thousand big old long horn steers and they would do nothing but mill around. The boss had given up in disgust and had gone up on a little hill to cool off. The steers were hot and the men were hot. I looked on for a moment and not a man made a move to stop the mill. I rode into them as they came around, cut off a bunch, and another man rode in behind me. That broke up the mill and they took the creek. In twenty minutes every steer was across into the herd.

The boss galloped up to me and said: "Do you want a job?" I told him I did and he told me to come on into camp. As we crossed I could see many dead cattle which had been tramped down in the mud. We rode into camp over on the next creek and the boss, Dick Withers, said he would give me $40 a month if I would ride my three horses and he would furnish me six other horses. In crossing the creek they had broken the hind axle of the wagon and had hauled it to camp with a pole under the axle tied up to the front axle. Mr. Withers asked if I knew anything about putting an axle in a wagon. I told him I didn't and he told me to go on herd. They cut down a small elm tree and one of the men went to another camp for tools and that afternon the wagon was fixed.

The men of the outfit were Dick Withers, the boss, George Lyons, Jake Fulgem, Frank Woods, Dave Richter, Ben Barker, Bill Hoskins, Nat Jackman, Dan Keen, E. N. Yates, George Kees, the cook, and Negro Albert. I was put on night herd with Negro Albert and stood from midnight until 2 o'clock. Yates, Richter, Barker and Shaw were the drag drivers and with this 1,800 head of yearlings that had been driven from the coast it was a very hard job. George Lyons was on the left point and Jake Fulgem on the right point.[11] We struck an old trail running from Fort Worth to Fort Dodge, Kan., and along this trail there were many carcasses of horses and old work oxen and these old oxen would be from 4 to 15 years old, with holes bored in their horns where the owner had blown in turpentine and salt to cause hollow horn. Dave Richter would gather the oldest of these horns, then catch one of the yearlings, bore a hole in the old horn with his knife and with rawhide string tie them on the yearling, then he would cut the bush of his tail off, as they do with work oxen. That would make about the funniest sight I ever saw.

Jake Fulgem would often come back when we would be two or three miles behind and help and the first time he got Mr. Withers back there he showed him a pair of them. In just a few days after that Mr. Sherrill came out to meet us. Mr. Withers was very enthusiastic over the little oxen with the big horns and told Mr. Sherrill that he must see them. Mr. Sherrill said he would go out and they got him a good horse and saddle and as Jake had worked for him he said, "Come on, Jake." I was on herd and Jake came to me and said, "We must find one of those yearlings with the ten-year-old horns." We strung the cattle out until we found one. Mr. Sherrill got a look at him and said, "Dick, this is only a yearling." Mr. Withers bet him a $10 hat. Mr. Sherrill said, "Dick, those horns are not natural." Withers wanted to bet more. Sherrill ordered Jake to catch the yearling, which he did. While the yearling was bucking the string broke and the horns were gone.

Mr. Withers said, "I owe every man in the bunch a treat." Mr. Sherrill brought out a big box of cigars and told all the men to help themselves. It was a large box and went very slow. I never had smoked any and did not wish to, but that night the cattle were lying quiet on the bedground. Albert and I always rode in opposite directions around the herd and after we had passed each other he turned and rode with me. "Mr. Shaw," he said, "how we gone keep even wid de other boys wid dem segars? Does you smoke?" I said that I didn't. "Needer does I," said Albert, "and dem other boys is smoking all de time." I said, "Well, Albert, I will tell you how we will do. It is no harm to smoke and you can go down and light one and come out smoking and I will take it and go round the herd until I meet you and you can take it again." Each night we did this until the cigars were all gone.

My second river was Wolf Creek which ordinarily was but a small creek, but this morning it was high, with big trees, washed out by the roots, coming down. When we drag drivers got up, the lead cattle were milling around and I noticed all the pointers and top men going around with them. I was so anxious to see what was ahead that I rode up and just about then Mr. Withers had cut a few head of the old work oxen and was having an awful time to hold them. He yelled at me to grab one of them and swim across. I was riding an old horse that had seen only one river, but I had no time to meditate. The yells and wild gestures of the boss knocked all notions out of my head, so I grabbed my rope and started beating one of the old steers until he was in swimming water. The steer and I floated down the river until we came out way down the stream. Mr.

Withers had driven two head across and he told me to hold them close to the bank, while he dropped into the river and swam to the other side. The boys by this time had cut off a bunch and had them in, and with a man on each side were fighting them across. All of the herd followed.

Then we had to get the wagons across. Sometimes in swimming the river we would pile the grub as high as we could and hitch four yoke of oxen, with a man to swim on each side and swim them across. The next river was Cold Creek. We got across it and were to deliver some yearlings there. We camped on the river bottom, which was a mile wide or more. Just about dark it began to rain and the boss asked me to take the horses out and hold them. About 9 o'clock there came a most terrific storm, with hail, rain and lightning striking all around us. While I was two miles away I could hear the cattle running. We had a small bulls-eye lantern, with a good hand-hold on the side and with a slide on it to cover up the light when it was not wanted. Just about when the cattle stampeded a light could be seen. Mr. Withers rode back to see what could be the matter. A horse was hitched to a small mesquite tree and the light appeared to be not more than eight feet from the ground, but was in the top of the tree. Mr. Withers hollered out, "Who in hell is up in that tree?" Bill Hoskins replied, "It's me, Mr. Withers." "I thought," said Mr. Withers, "that you were the only damn fool that would not have sense enough to turn his light out after climbing a tree."

Bill was from Virginia and had never seen a cow herd until he had seen that one and he was the biggest coward I ever saw, although he was always anxious to tell us that he was one of the F. F. V.'s of Pocahontas blood.[12]

The next river was the Red River and when we got to it it looked to be a mile wide, but it was not swimming deep except for a short distance. There were three channels that were swimming, but when I reached the river the cattle were going in nicely and the only trouble we had was when some of the cattle bogged and we had to pull them out. Dave Richter got sick, could not eat anything, and in the evening George Kees told me to kill a rabbit and he would make Dave some soup. I could not get a rabbit, but shot a prairie dog and some soup was made from that for Dave.[13] A day or two after this Richter and Kees had a fight in which Kees was shot and both he and Richter were sent to Fort Reno and from there sent back home. I was so far behind with the drags that I had not heard of the fight or saw the boys go away. When we got up to about a mile of camp I went to the wagon to get a drink and there were three men in camp. Frank Woods stepped up and threw a six-shooter down between my eyes and said: "Did you tell Mr. Withers that I cut that herd in two?" "No," I said, "I have not seen Mr. Withers since morning."

Just then George Lyons, who was sitting at the hind wheel of the wagon, grabbed his Winchester and taking aim at Woods, said: "Drop it, or I will

38

bust your head open." Woods fell back out of sight and was gone. The quarrel was about cutting the herd in two.[14] A few days after this we were going across a very dry country in Indian Territory, north of the Wichita hills, and the herd had no water for two days. There was just a small breeze from the west, but the cattle smelled water and as I looked ahead I could see the men working diligently and fast with the lead cattle, but with little success. The men from further down the line ran as fast as they could to help, but about a thousand head of big long-horn cattle had smelled the water that the breeze had wafted toward them. They were bawling, switching their tails and clashing their horns together and were gradually gaining ground on the men. They would mill for a time and stand with heads down and bawl as if they were deliberating. I asked the man next to me if we should not go and help. Ned Yates said, "I think we will have enough to do here if we ever get this end up to there."

The herd was strung out about two miles long, but the lead was on high ground and we could not see it all. The men worked hard and fast, but the cattle were gaining ground. All of the herd was then running, except the extreme tail end, and these were walking fast. Every cow seemed to know that there was something wrong. They had all smelled the water in the Wichita River by this time and, as one cowboy expressed it, "had hell in their necks." All down the line, to the little dogey, every animal had started to bawl, with that sad and lonely bawl the cowboys know so well. The country sloped toward the river, and as the cattle made one fast turn, with their tails high in the air and their horns clashing together, there was no use trying to stop them. It was a plain case of electricity working among them from one to another.

The boss had come up by this time and waved us to stop and later waved for us to come to him. Mr. Withers had sent a man ahead to stop the wagon and we made a dry camp there. We got some rest that afternoon. This was a high, level or more or less rolling country, but along the river it was very rough and full of wild turkey and deer. The boss rolled us out at half past 3 and at 4 we were making toward the river. The roundup was well managed and at 10 we had the cattle on the trail. Then we had to count. We found we were short at least 400 head.

The boss had sent men back and all through the brush, so that it was a sure thing the cattle had been driven up the river. These boys were good hands and could trail cattle and tell buffalo tracks from cow tracks and they could tell whether cattle had been driven or not. They reported that there were ten men driving the cattle at a fast gait. Then the boss sent four men after them and we started the herd for the river, about eight miles away. We got in on the North Canadian River and were getting our dinner when the four men came in.

They reported that they had found the cattle and also that they saw fifteen teepees on the Wichita River and as they started for the cattle they saw fifteen Indians come out of the teepees with guns in their hands. There was a government interpreter, licensed by the army, just up the river with another herd that had had trouble and the boss sent for him and told him our trouble. The interpreter said he knew all of these Indians and that he could talk to them. "I will get the cattle back," he said, "but you must send three good men with me." The boss sent Jake Fulgem, Bill Hoskins and myself back with him. The Washataw and the Wichita come together here and between the rivers was about the prettiest valley I ever saw. As we rode across the river toward the teepees the chief, Old Spotted Horse, rode to meet us. We stopped in the river to water our horses and when the chief came up to the interpreter he told him they had the cattle and had killed five of them, as they were awful hungry and had to eat. The interpreter told him it was all O. K. and said for us to tell him it was all right. The chief came back to shake hands with us and told us in signs that he had killed the beef. We each told him that was good and he seemed to be satisfied and motioned to us to fol-low and he ran on ahead. Old Spotted Horse went to the teepees and told the warriors it was all right. An old squaw ran to a hill and yelled like a panther and made a sign by throwing a blanket above her head and off to one side. She did this three times, when an old buck came out of the breaks, carrying on old cap and ball rifle, the pieces of which were tied together with string. He laid the gun down and came up to shake hands with each of us and seemed tickled to death. Just behind him came three squaws leading three ponies. The three beeves were tied up in three beef hides and packed on the ponies. They rolled them off on the grass and spread the hides, put the beef on them and went to work. They had strings stretched from tree to tree and would cut the meat in strips about a foot long and hang it over a rawhide string to dry in the sun. There was a big pot of beef on the fire boiling and the old buck taking care of it. The chief was busy showing us his pass and this is what was on it: "This is a good Indian. Let him pass and repass." Army officers' names were signed to it. By this time the beef was done and the old buck set it off and poured a half bucket of cold water on it. Then he stuck his hand in the pot and handed each of us a piece. It looked as though he had never washed his hands. The interpreter ate his and told us to eat, that we would get nothing more until we got back to the wagon. When we left the wagon the boss had told us to hurry, as he could not lay over and had to travel, and that we would have to catch up as best we could. The Indians had brought the cattle close to camp and we went out to them. The chief told the interpreter that he would charge us ten head for gathering and holding them and said they caught them several miles down the trail running back south. Jake asked me what we should do and I told him to go in and cut out every old bull and lame yearling in the bunch. This he did and we started out. The Indians asked us to give them two heifer yearlings and they would hold them for us that night. They made signs that cowboy was tired and would go to sleep and cattle get away. "We are cowboys and we can hold them and we must be going," we told them.

We crossed the river and drove along. The cattle had been well grassed and watered and were content to lie down. Jake had been alkalied in the Indian Territory—in fact we all had been, but most of us had gotten over it.[15] I said that I would stand guard until 1 o'clock and Bill could stand until 3 and then we would start out. I stood until 1 and then put Bill on. I got up about 3 and neither Bill nor the cattle could be found. I awakened the interpreter who said to lie down until daylight and we would go out and get them again.

We started out after it grew light. The interpreter said for Jake and I to look up the river and he would take Bill as he had the best horse. Jake and I rode all around and could find only the trail where the cattle went. The interpreter took the trail and we went and lay down in the shade. We had some coffee and a quart cup with a handle, but the coffee was all we had in the way of something to eat, and we were hungry. I crossed the river and went to the teepees and visited around until I found that all the bucks were gone, and I knew they were after the cattle. I found one buck and two kids in a teepee asleep. To be a good mixer in an Indian camp you must help yourself, so I raised the flap of the teepee and went in. I could see that the old buck did not want me, but the two boys seemed delighted. One boy was about

43

16 and he at once began to show me things and seemed real glad to entertain me, but the old buck would make signs with his hands like a horse galloping and point south.

I thought I had my pistol under my arm, but the first thing I knew the young buck had it and was making out the door. I made a jump for him and got the gun, which I then held in my hand. I told the old buck to go to camp with me. I made signs that I had a sick man over the river and waived my pistol around in a threatening manner. He stuck his head out of the teepee and told a squaw to bring his pony. He mounted and we started. As we passed out I chewed my finger and made a motion toward the meat on the line. The squaw laughed and handed me as much as I wanted.

I went to the shade where Jake was and made the coffee and broiled some of the meat on a stick. Jake drank a little coffee and ate some of the meat. I ate the meat and drank water, saving the coffee for the other man. The Indian made signs that riding in the hot sun had made his head ache and he wanted some of the coffee. I told Jake what the fellow wanted and Jake said that if that "copper-colored damned ———"put his mouth to the coffee to kill him. I think the Indian understood what Jake said, for just then he got in a hurry to go and I rode out with him and let him go.

About 10 o'clock the men came with the cattle and I never let them stop. We left the two tired riders two of the horses and what we had to eat and took the cattle. We reached the Canadian River about dark and Bill and the interpreter had just got to us. The interpreter never stopped, but went right on to the herd. The herd was a day and a half ahead of us, but it was moonlight that night and when we got the cattle on the trail it was easy going, being a level country and no timber.

About 10 o'clock we heard a man shouting. We answered and shot and I could see a man coming on the run. It was E. N. Yates, with a bucket of grub. I can say for a fact that was the best grub I ever ate. We never allowed the cattle to stop and it was surprising how they trailed that night. Just as it began to grow gray in the east we turned them into the herd. Jake and I turned our horses loose and lay down and slept for about an hour.

Bill was more scared by an Indian than any man I ever knew. As we came down to the river that night I was up in the lead and gave Jake the job of driving along behind us, as that would be easy on him, and Bill was to take the other side. I could see that his side was losing and I told Jake I didn't believe Bill was turning the cattle in on the trail. Bill was then riding close to Jake and Jake told him not to let the cattle scatter out too far, but to go around and turn them in on the trail. Bill said: "I'll be damned if I am going to set myself for a target to be shot at." Jake ran up to him and jerked out his pistol and said: "If you don't 'round them cattle I'll bend this iron round your head." That was the last time Bill had to be told to go around them.

45

George Lyons was a good friend of mine from the start and when he drew the Winchester on Woods when he had a pistol in my face I considered it a very great favor, and I told him so. One night when we were in Texas he rode up to me when my guard was about half out and said: "Say, Jim, there are two deputy sheriffs in camp from Williamson County, looking for a horse thief." I commenced to laugh and he got mad and said a cuss word or two. I ran after him and thanked him and got him in a good humor. Lyons was assistant trail boss. When we got into Kansas we had all kinds of trouble with the new settlers. They would plow a furrow and if we crossed over that they would have us pulled and fined and under no consideration would they allow us to cross unless it was time to bed the cattle and then they would give us all kinds of inducements to camp on their land, so they could use the buffalo chips for fuel the next winter. They would guard them like a Texas man does a watermelon patch, until they were ripe enough to haul in. We never saw a stick of wood for days in Kansas and had to use buffalo chips to cook with.

One evening we pulled in on the Arkansas River two miles above Fort Dodge and there was a most beautiful little town called Dodge City just across the river from our camp.[16] That night it rained and the cattle stampeded, but after an hour or so we got them stopped and Yates and myself, George Lyons and Albert were the men on the job. If any of the others got out we never saw them. The boss asked who we were and we told him, as it was so dark we could not see. He said, "You boys go up to that dobie house and lie down until daylight, and be sure you get inside for fear the cattle get to running and trample you to death."[17] Next morning about 10 o'clock I could see nobody around but Negro Albert on herd with me. I rode up to interrogate Albert and he said the others had all gone to town. Two men with 4,800 head of cattle and 70 head of horses was rather light, but we had not much trouble in the morning. We grazed them toward the river and let them go to water as they liked, but at noon we had nothing to eat and had to round up and catch a change of horses as best we could. We could not be together, as one had to be with the cattle all the time.

About the middle of the afternoon the big steers wanted to travel and then we had our troubles. It seemed as if they were just bound to go and they got out two miles past camp, but fortunately some of the men came back and came to our assistance. The boss got back by this time and Albert and I went to camp, where we found a black Negro cooking supper. Jake rode in and started to get off his horse, but fell off. A boy caught and unsaddled the horse and Jake sat up against the wagon wheel. Albert said, "Where do you suppose dem cattle would abin if Mr. Shaw and me had went to town?" Jake was drunk, but he knew it was aimed at him. He raised up, knocked the shells out of his pistol and put in cartridges and said: "It's all right, ain't it, Albert?" Albert answered, "Yes, sah, cose it is." Jake laughed until you could hear him all over camp.

47

It was dark then and the boss came to me and said, "Jim, I have bought 25 head of new horses and put them in the bunch. Will you take them out and hold them for me?" I told him I would if he would give me three fresh ones to ride and catch the best one for me to ride that night. He was very anxious about them and cautioned me not to lose one of them. I brought them all in about half past 3 o'clock.

The Arkansas was not swimming and we had no trouble in crossing. After we had got the wagons over the boss told me that I could go to town if I desired. I rode in and saw a very pretty town of about 400 inhabitants. Every year there would be a few men killed there and of course the police were on the watch. As I rode in the marshal stopped to look at me and turned into a saloon, which was wide open.[18] I hitched my horse and as I walked by going to a store I saw the marshal drinking with several other men and a little woman by his side. He was a strong looking man, weighing about 200 pounds, while she was a small woman. As she turned around to come out I could see that her face and hands were bloody and there was a scar on her head. I saw the men in the store looking at them and I asked what was the matter. They said the man and woman had quarreled and he had hit her with his pistol. I was anxious to get out of Dodge City.

It rained all morning and we camped six miles out on a creek called Sawlog. The negro cook had driven the mess wagon in to load up with grub enough to take us to Ogallala. The boss hurried him

48

Shaw' Trail 1879

49

out and as he pulled into camp one or two of the cowboys who had fallen by the wayside the night before rolled out of the wagon. It rained most of the day and we pulled about six miles that afternoon. We were now among people who had settled there that spring. The boss had sold a man a yoke of oxen and told me to get them out for him. I roped the steers and tied them to a wheel. It was black land and awfully muddy. The tallest man I ever saw came up with his pants rolled up to his knees and barefooted. He had a girl with him and she had her skirts to fit the fashions nowadays and was also barefooted. I went with him for a short distance, but he said he could manage them, that he could outrun them anywhere.

After we left this settlement we saw nothing until we came to a little town called Buffalo. Then there was nothing more until we came to Ogallala, Neb. George Lyons, George Kees and Bill Hoskins went back to Texas from Dodge City. Kees was a good cook, but with Negro John we got nothing to eat. We crossed three rivers from there to Ogallala, the Dismal, the Blue and I do not remember the other one. On one of them we got the finest plums I ever saw. We camped just a few miles below Ogallala and the old boss came around and said, "Boys, I don't want any of you to go to town. The men are here to receive these cattle and we will be awful busy working them tomorrow and I want you to be strong and active." Then he came to me privately and said, "You can go to town if you wish, as you are not liable to get drunk and be unable to work tomorrow."[19]

Ogallala consisted of a good hotel, a little log cabin for a store, and four saloons and a good looking depot. All of the saloons were on the south side of the Union Pacific railroad and were two stories high, with rooms above, and were good looking buildings. There I met Dave Lygon, who had been in the Ranger service in Texas and had served two years as a deputy sheriff at Austin. We were soon well acquainted. We went to the little store and bought what we wanted and then went to the other side to see what we could see. We went into the first one, then to the second and third, and there was nobody there. In the fourth one the men were all there. There were several small games going and at one table there was a big game going on, with more money than I had ever seen on the table. We of course were anxious to see and walked up to look. There was a short, stout looking man just opposite us, with a large pile of bills and a white-handled pistol on top of them. The man looked up and said, "Is that you, Dave?" Dave said, "Yes, Howdy, Billie?" Billie said, "Dave, I'll give you ten minutes to get out of here." Dave just seemed to be very busy looking over the man's pile of money. "Did you hear me, Dave?" said Billie. Dave said, "Now, Billie, you know that I am not going to be run out of here." Billie had taken hold of his pistol and uttering a cuss word, he said, "I'll kill you before you have a chance to get out." I grabbed Dave by the arm and ran for the door, which was only forty feet away but seemed at least 200 yards. I ran with Dave as fast as I could, and he was not much trouble to lead, either. I never stopped until we got on our horses and then I asked Dave who his friend was. "Bill Thompson," said Dave, "didn't you know him? When I was deputy sheriff I put him in jail three times."

We grassed out about three miles next morning. The famous Dick Head, one of the best cattlemen that ever came from Texas, had charge of all of Sherrill & Ellison's herds after we got to Ogallala.[20] All of the big steers were sold and delivered there. The she stock was sold to Captain Bronson and we had to deliver them to him at the Bosler pens on Running Water.[21] A thousand head of the steer yearlings were to be delivered to F. E. Warren and Guiterman on Warbonnet in South Dakota.[22]

Mr. Head soon convinced me that he was a first class man. He mounted himself and some others on good horses and started cutting out the big steers. About the second animal he cut out was a mad bull, running him through and out of the herd. He told me and another man to tie him down. The bull was furious and we had to be careful. Those Spanish bulls have long horns and are very active. I rode up close enough for him to charge me and the other man rode close enough to catch him. I caught him by the hind foot and we tied him down. I held him by the hind foot while the other man tied him. Mr. Head was busy cutting cattle and in a few moments the bull got up and almost caught him. Mr. Head was both mad and scared and he came toward us using some very bad and very expressive language, but this man of his knew him and never stopped to listen to what he had to say, but rode up and caught the bull. That time we tied him so that he was there the last I saw of him.

Mr. Head was a large, good looking man, with a very black beard and eyes that seemed to penetrate you. He asked me to help him and I was glad to be able to do so. Then we began to cut the steers into bunches, 2 to 5 in a bunch, cutting all of the she stuff in one bunch toward the south and the big steers to the north. Mr. Sherrill and another man were working on the south side of the herd, cutting the she stuff. Mr. Sherrill was an old man and a stranger to that kind of work, but seemed to me to be anxious that Mr. Head should think him just at home there. I could see that Mr. Head expected me to do most of the work, although he said but little to me, but we worked fast and by dinner time had the herd about all cut to pieces. All of the steers from 2-year-olds up were in one bunch, the she stuff in another, leaving the yearlings in a third bunch. I never got to see the big steers any more, but when I got back from dinner Mr. Head asked me if I was riding a good horse. Then he told me he was going to take out the cows and heifer yearlings and wanted me to hold them up for him. "I will start out the first bunch," he said, "and after they are tallied we will drive them out about a quarter of a mile and I will put two men to watch them. After that you are to ride in the lead of each bunch and don't let any bunch go until I wave my handkerchief."

These cows and yearling heifers were being delivered to Mr. Bronson. I think he had been a captain in the army. They were counting and classing at the same time. All of the 2-year-old heifers went the same as cows at $15 a head, while the yearlings were being sold at $10 a head.

While I was sorry for Mr. Bronson I was many times amused. I was where I could hear every word that was said and I was sure from the first that Bronson had never classed cattle before, and there he was classing with one of the fastest cattlemen that ever came over the trail. In the first place it was hard for Bronson in a big rush, when the cattle were running, for him to tell a yearling from a 2-year-old. They would cut out a bunch, some times as many as fifty head, and the men would have to hurry them to get them out of the bunch. Then Head would call out "35 cows and 15 yearlings." Then is when I would have to show my skill, for I would have to hold the bunch until the dispute was settled. Mr. Head would tell Bronson that he was the slowest classer he had ever worked with and many other things to make Bronson feel small, and sometimes cuss him until Bronson would give in and let the bunch go through. I think Bronson lost about $5,000 that day.

The cows had to be delivered to Mr. Bronson at the Bosler pens on Running Water in Nebraska and the yearling steers on Warbonnet in South Dakota. The next morning we had to say farewell to our old Texas cowboys, or most of them, Nat Jackman,

Jake Fulgem, Frank Woods, Albert and Mr. Withers. We crossed the South Platte and had no trouble except for quicksand. We crossed the Union Pacific railroad and bid farewell to Ogallala.

Then for a few days we had Mr. Head for a boss, and he did not mind telling his experiences, trials and troubles, which were many. He had gone from Southern Texas to California with a trail herd and to hear him tell about it was better than anything I had ever heard. We came over and crossed the North Platte river and traveled up it to Camp Clark and there crossed to the east side to the Bosler pens in Nebraska. There we delivered the cows and Mr. Head and all of the old men except Yates and Ben Barker went back to Ogallala. Then with Mr. Pierce as boss and with Negro John and a pack outfit we started for the Bar Circle ranch on Warbonnet. We left the famous old mess wagon and oxen with Mr. Bronson. That was another lonesome day. All of the Texas men went back from there except Ned Yates, Ben Barker and myself. There were two men hired at Dodge City, but I do not remember their names. Ned Yates christened one of them Lousy Joe and that name followed him through, and just fit him, so far as I could make out.

There was another outfit that traveled with us all the way through, driven by Jake de Poysture. He was driving for the Shiners. Jake was with us at Ogallala. He was eating supper one evening when a telegram was given him that said: "Bill Ward killed Alveno." Jake jumped for his horse and ran for his camp,

55

which was then near Big Springs. They brought the dead Mexican to Ogallala and Lousy Joe quit his job to sit up with the corpse, as they offered him $5 to sit up with the corpse and prepare it for burial.

In going up the North Platte when we got within fifty miles of Fort Laramie I was very anxious to hunt up Tom Shaw, and I knew from what he had said about Fort Laramie that I would find him from there. So I went to Mr. Head and told him all about the situation as nicely as I could. Mr. Head came back at me in the most diplomatic way. He said: "Now, Mr. Shaw, I appreciate the situation and I am awfully sorry that I cannot comply with your wishes, but you see I have your record, your ability and your faithfulness to us all the way from Texas, and that is the reason that I have selected you for the very important position of helping me deliver the last of this herd to our customers up north. Now, be a good fellow and help me finish delivering and I will remember it and if you ever want anything and it is in my power you can have it." I said: "You win," and went back to the herd.

MR. PIERCE was a one-horse sort of a fellow and I quarreled with him twice. We landed on White River, three miles below Fort Robinson,[23] on the fifth day from the Bosler pens. Joe Willis and I were left on herd. The yearlings were crossing as good as we could wish and Joe and I went up to the Fort. We went into a place and got a bottle of beer and sat under a shade tree and drank it, as we were very thirsty. As we rode around looking at things we went across the parade ground, which was very offensive to the commanding officer. Twelve men stepped out of the soldiers' quarters and with guns ordered us to halt. Of all the fast riding that was ever done we did it then. The soldiers used good judgment and did not fire on us, but we never stopped running until we got to camp. There was a road ranch on the White River where Crawford now stands and the little outfit got dinner there that day. The road ranch was run by Jack Talbert and Tobacco Jake. That night we camped at another road ranch on Cottonwood Creek and there a man by the name of Louie Green met us to pilot us to the ranch. He gave Mr. Pierce directions to get to the ranch and also gave me directions how to take the cattle. There was no road, but there was a large mud hill that we could see for miles and he told us to "go right by the hill but not to go around it, and as you go past it you will notice a small creek that heads there and you go down that creek and you will find plenty of grass and water. Then all you have to do is to keep a sharp watch to see that no buffalo get among the cattle, for if they do they will stampede the herd."

We got there fairly well with the lead cattle and I left Joe to watch them while I went back to help Ned and Ben with the others. Mr. Pierce came up about 8 o'clock with the pack, the negro cook and the horses, and asked me if I thought I could follow the directions. I told him I thought I could and then he told me what Louie Green had told him, to bear just around the mountain and take down the first creek. I knew he was going to get lost, but I said not a word, for I knew it would bring on another argument. There were no roads and the other boys wanted to follow the horse tracks, but I told them that I was sure that I was right.

We got the last of the cattle on the water about 2 o'clock but we had no change of horses, no camp and nothing to eat. We lay under the shade of a cotton-wood tree and had a good sleep. Mr. Pierce came up about 5 o'clock, the maddest man I ever saw. He simply cussed a blue streak, said that we were off the way, that he was on the right road and that it was about nine miles to his camp. He said that Negro John had cooked up the last batch of our grub and we would have to drive the cattle over there. Then he asked who directed the herd this way and some one said that I had. He told me to get up and start the cattle to camp, but I told him Green had directed me down this creek and I was not going to drive them any other way.

Then I expected him to shoot me, but I was ready for him and he knew it. Then he said we must have the horses and cattle together. "Who will go with me to bring the horses here?" he asked. No one said anything for a time and finally Ben said he would go. At about dark we bedded the cattle, but there was nothing to eat and no change of horses. The horses and the cook got in about 10 o'clock and John made some coffee. The cook had had fried corn cakes and bacon at the other camp, but had put it in a sack and it was badly mixed up. We caught our night horses and I went out and around the cattle and they were doing nicely. The only thing we had to fear was that the buffalo would stampede them.

I got up early and brought in the horses and the boys caught their mounts. We had nothing to do but go, as we had nothing to eat. I started the cattle down the creek and in about an hour I met Green and he said: "You got in early." I said: "Where is the ranch?" He said: "Right here." And we were right at it.

We put the cattle in a large corral and got breakfast and then started to brand them. These cattle were delivered to F. E. Warren and Guiterman and Mr. Guiterman was there to receive them. Louie Green was the ranking cowboy and asked: "Who is the best roper?" Ben Barker said that John was. I said: "I guess I will not wrestle and let the negro rope. I will rope."[24] We had to pull and drag them up like branding calves and the wrestlers held them by the hind legs. A yearling hooked his foot into Ned Yates' shirt and kicked it off of him and I never heard a man cuss like Ned did, for it was all he had and Cheyenne was our nearest town. Mr. Guiterman seriously objected to swearing, as it was Sunday, but Ned cussed all the louder. Mr. Guiterman said a man could not swear on his premises on Sunday. Ned then said: "You better put off your branding until tomorrow, for I am liable to swear any time." Then Guiterman said: "Go ahead with the work and swear all you like, young man."

We finished branding the next day and went up the creek and bathed and cleaned up and put on our best clothes, which were not much. This looked to me to be an ideal cow range and the best grass I ever saw. There was plenty of game, such as antelope, deer and buffalo. The next morning, September 15,

1879, we took our departure. I did not mind parting with the little steers, but, oh, how I hated to part with the old horses. We started for the Pine Ridge Indian reservation, Ned, Ben, Joe, Negro John and I. Mr. Guiterman gave us some coffee, bread and bacon, but said they could not spare much, as they had but little on the ranch. We went along until about noon and then stopped to have our lunch and let our horses rest, and as this was about the first time we had been off herd, day and night, for a long time we lay down and took a good sleep. In the afternoon we started again, going along a draw. All we had to go by was the directions we had received. We were to hit White River at the mouth of Bordeaux Creek and there we would find a ranch. I went ahead and the boys drove the horses after me and after awhile the boys reported that John was missing. We waited and one of the boys rode back but could see nothing of him. That was the last we ever did see of Negro John.

The ranch in question was on the opposite bank of the river from us and there being some heavy timber along there we missed it. That night when we unpacked we found that John had gone through our pack at noon and taken what he wanted and had got lost on purpose. There was nothing in the pack that could be considered valuable, but I had an old dictionary that I had had through school and a small Bible that had been given me by a very dear friend, with a photograph and a few lines that I prized very highly. John could not read, but he had been away

61

from civilization so long that I suppose he thought he had better practice a little for fear he would lose the art of stealing.

That night we camped on White River and ate the last bit of grub that we had. While I was hobbling the horses the fire broke out and we almost lost all of our clothes trying to stop it. I then cautioned the boys and told them that if we let the fire get out the Indians would kill every one of us, as we were then on an Indian reservation.

The next morning was the 17th of September. We had a cup of coffee, but that was all. All that day we traveled, but saw no signs of inhabitants. Every time we crossed the White River our pack horse bogged down and we had to wade in and pack out. That night we camped with nothing to eat. The next day we started and again the deer and the antelope were so wild that we could not get close enough to get a shot at them. We found out that the Indians had been hunting through there.

About 5 o'clock we found lots of Indian graves, with dead Indians buried in trees. The red blankets looked good and we threw out some of them, but they were rotten. With each of the warriors would be some kind of a metal dishpan or a terrapin shell where they had left grub for him. The mice and the birds had eaten the grub, but the shell would be there, with the tin spoon in it. You can talk about fancy work, but I saw some of it there. The grown Indians would be laid on sticks in the trees, but the little babies would be in the nicest little beds, with the willows bent over them like a basket and the willow twigs would be put over them until the water could not get through. They were all tied at the bottom with strings or willow twigs. A great many of them had been blown down and there were heads and other bones scattered all over the place. I was rather glad that we did not get any of the blankets when they told us at the reservation that smallpox had hit them along the river in 1876—killed off lots of them.

We camped on White River again, with nothing to eat. The next morning we thought the river was going too far north, so we crossed and started south, climbing some high hills, and about noon we got on a high hill so that we could see all down the country to the east. After looking for a long time we saw smoke and we were a happy lot of men. The smoke proved to be about ten miles away and we made for it and it proved to be Camp Sheridan.[25]

We reached the camp about 4 o'clock, being 48 hours with nothing to eat. We camped and I sent Joe to get some bread while I got some lard and a number of slices of beef. We had a feast and laid down to sleep. When Joe came back with the bread he had a gunny sack full, carrying it on his shoulder like a sack of oats. The next morning, we rode into the Pine Ridge Agency. This was a nice morning and all the little Indians had gone out to play up a nice, big draw. There were about 300 of them and as they came down the hill they stampeded and of all the sights in my life, it was about the best. They were boys from 2 to 12 years of age. The banks were rather steep and the big boys in their rush for safety ran over the little ones.

We went to the sutler's store and he told us we would have to notify the agent of what we wanted and make arrangements to stay on the reservation or the Indian police would put us off. The agent's office was about 300 yards away. I went down, but the agent's clerk was all I could find, as the agent had gone out in the country. As I went down to the agent's office three big Indians trailed along behind me. Just then the clerk was busy and told me to wait a moment. I sat down and I noticed that the Indians all stopped outside of the building. One of them had the biggest nose that I had ever seen, and it appears that he was the one to watch me. I sat there and that Indian would look in and the moment he saw me watching him he would dodge back, but that nose would soon appear around the door facing, just ahead of a big black eye.

The clerk called me to a window and I told him my business and said that I wanted a permit to remain around for a few days. He said he did not think that necessary, but he said he would sign the agent's name to a piece of paper and hand it to me and those Indians who followed me would see him hand it to me and that would be all I needed. The Indians followed me back and wherever I went kept close watch on me. I told the boys that they found something in my makeup that I had never found out yet.

A man was in from the camp on Wounded Knee and we followed him out and camped there and found the foreman, a man by the name of Sam Fowler. He told us that Mr. Newman had gone to Chicago and left no word with him for us and it would just be impossible for him to give one of us work, for none of his men had quit or shown signs of quitting. He said that Mr. Newman had a cow camp 50 miles south of us and as he went by there when he went away he might have left some word at that place. Next morning we started for this ranch, 50 miles south on Running Water and the only directions they could give us was to go straight south and this was very indefinite. The route was through the sandhills and it was Indian summer, so that we could not see more than a few miles. In starting out from the camp on Wounded Knee, Ben Barker went over to talk to one of the cowboys and that was the last we saw of him.

The day we spent at the camp was a great day for me. They called it the Pine Ridge Agency and it was new, having been established in 1878. It was then cold at night, so that beef would keep for a few days at a time and they were delivering every ten days. This delivery of beef was one of the best sights I have ever had the pleasure of seeing. The agent's clerk would call out the name of the family that was to have beef and the cowboys would run a longhorn steer out at the gate. Outside of the corral there would be about a hundred warriors, all painted up with war paint and riding their war horses bareback, with a string in the horse's mouth for a bridle, and armed with a Winchester, just as if they were going to war.

When the steer would get about 200 feet from the corral the chief would let out a yell and all of them would make a rush for the animal. Each of them would shoot at the steer. Sometimes they would run him five miles before they could kill him. All of the warriors would rush back and tell the squaws where they had left the steer and they would go and skin him and bring the meat back to camp. Then the clerk, on a high board over the gate, would call out another family's name and out would come another steer and the yelling and the fun would begin again. I heard that the Indians got to "playing white man" by shooting at some other Indian while the fun was going on and the Indian department changed the plan of delivery. At that time the United States was trying to teach the aborigine how to farm and had issued all kinds of farming machinery. At this time the Indians were haying. They would take the lines and split them in the middle and tie one end around the pony's neck and hold on to it or let it drag after the pony so he could catch him in the bunch. When he hitched up the team to mow he would put a little Indian on each pony and the same way when he started to haul hay. When the team started to go down hill one little Indian would signal to his brother on the other horse that the wagon was trying to catch up with them and each would try to make his horse outrun the wagon. When the wagon would bound when it hit the bottom the hay would go high in the air and the team would pull the wagon away before the hay got back.

Our government was then holding 4,000 steers, all large and matured steers, that it expected to deliver within the next year. Mr. Newman of Fort Worth, Tex., had the contract at the time and had lots of cattle both in Nebraska and Texas, but in 1903 I saw him in Wyoming selling Mexican cattle and he told me that he was "flat busted."

In going south to the ranch on Running Water we followed up the Wounded Knee for several miles, but as it seemed to lead us to the west we quit it and struck as near south as we could guess. In a very rough country as we were leaving Wounded Knee, where we did not imagine there was a human being within miles of us, a buck Indian pulled up in front of us, riding a very pretty yellow pony. We all thought he would give us some direction toward the ranch, but to any sign or any language we could use he would shake his head. He would pat his pony on the neck and point to Ned Yates' white-handled six-shooter and say "swap." We could understand that he wanted to trade the pony for Ned's gun, which would look like a good trade, but at that time a man felt pretty lonesome in that country without armament. After Ned had tried in vain to get something out of him he said: "I will give you the contents of the pistol directly." I believe that the Indian knew every word that Ned had said to him, as he jerked the pony around and jumped him off the bank of the creek and was gone. We had been warned against roving bands of Indians, as they had killed two cowboys in the sandhills a few days before.

We went ahead through a very rough country and struck a lake that seemed to have no end to it and was a half mile across. We went to the east around it and then south again. Then we stopped for a short rest for our horses, but we had nothing to eat. We could see antelope everywhere and worlds of fish, ducks and geese in the lake. We went south again and after a few miles we struck cattle, which was encouraging, but we could not locate the ranch or locate Running Water. At dark we camped. The next morning we saw one of the men from the ranch, who was hunting horses, and he directed us to the ranch.

We met the foreman at the ranch and he said that Mr. Newman had come by on his way east, but he had left no word for us. This man was kind enough to ask us to stay there until our horses rested up. The second day Ned and Joe went down to the spring house and found half a dozen pies. They had never seen a pie and did not know that they were a great delicacy, so ate them all up. The old cook then asked us to please move.

All the time we were there we had been debating as to what would be our next move. In the morning Ned said he was going south and Joe said that he was going with him. That left me alone. That was a sad hour for me, but I braced up and started for Fort Laramie. Ned and Joe went down the little river in an effort to get back to the Union Pacific railway so they could get a ticket back to Texas. In those days the famous Alex Swan had the Union Pacific issue tickets, first class, including stopovers, to cowboys in all points in Texas and return for $65.[26]

The first night I got to the ranch Joe Brazil was running the outfit, a good, lively Texas cowboy. There I had to leave one of my horses. The next night I got to the H3 ranch, owned by Jess Ivins and the foreman was Bob Ford. Bob was born in South Carolina but raised in Texas, about as fine a looking man as I ever knew and could play the fiddle to beat all. The next night I stopped at the 33 ranch. I asked for work at all of these ranches, but they were all full-handed.

The next night I got to Fort Laramie, but not a word could I hear of my brother, Tom. I found where Bordeaux was and knew that Tom got his mail there. I camped that night at the Six Mile ranch and the next night at Bordeaux.[27] There I sold a fine mare for $30. I had bought her from Woods and I always thought that he had stolen her, but I gave him $25 for her and she developed into a fine saddle animal. They told me at Bordeaux that Tom Shaw got his mail there and they thought he was working on the Laramie River. I made for the Laramie River and found Billy Bacon, who was running a road ranch at what afterward was named Uva. Billy told me all about Tom and just how to find him. I camped on the North Laramie River that night, near the HR ranch.

Mr. Heck Reel was at the ranch and asked me over and talked to me about the trail work and how we did it when we got to Ogallala.[28] I told all about it and he said to his foreman, Ves Sherman: "Hire this man, Ves. I want at least one good man on this ranch." I had the appearance of a man about 40, for I had whiskers on, not having shaved since I left home in Texas. After I had gone to work for the HR outfit Ves told me I had made a good impression on Mr. Reel. The next day they wanted to send a man to tell the Duck outfit that they were going to round-up toward Fort Laramie and I told them that I would take the message.

My anticipation of meeting my brother, Tom, was at fever heat and on going over I met him on the road. I worked at the HR ranch about six weeks and then they formed an association to hire men and put them between the Platte and the Laramie Rivers to push back cattle and keep them from the Fort and from going into Goshen Hole. Jim Carroll and I were stationed on the Laramie and Louie St. Clair and Sam Moses on the Platte. We worked as faithfully as we could, but the cattle increased in numbers every day until it was impossible for us to handle them. We went to Mr. Whitman and Mr. Sawyer, who owned cattle on the ranges, and they talked with the others and they called us off on Christmas Day, 1879.

I went to see my brother, Tom, on the Duck ranch on Cottonwood and John Rees, who was foreman, told me I could stay there and hunt and kill

70

game for the ranch until work opened up and then they would give me a job. Some time about the 1st of January, 1880, we planned a hunt and went over on the edge of the Laramie Plains to kill enough meat to do us until Spring. We loaded a wagon with a tent, grub and corn for our horses and started out. The hills were snowed over and the horses not shod. We got stuck and had to unload all of our junk and make about three trips to get out. There was plenty of snow, the wind was blowing and it was cold, but we camped in the pine forest and built up about the biggest fire I ever saw. There was Fred deBillier, H. E. Teschemacher, Tom Shaw and myself.[29] We ate and sat around the fire until time to go to bed. We had staked the tent, shoveled out the snow and rolled out our beds and turned in, but there was no sleep for poor Tom. I never saw anyone suffer like he did that night with chilblains on his feet. He would go to sleep and then he would almost jump out of his bed. About midnight he got up and walked barefooted through the snow, dried his feet on a saddle blanket, got into bed and went to sleep.

Next morning we started out early and got over on the Laramie Plains to Frank Preager's cabin.[30] Frank was at home and asked us in. We declined his kind offer, but took rather kindly to his fresh elk meat and would go in the cabin in the evening and hear him talk. Frank was a bachelor of about 40 years and had had many adventures with Indians. We wondered how he had lived in this country so many years and still had his scalp and then he would branch out and tell a few things that would make your hair stand. Preager showed us a small cabin in the yard, the first one he had built. One evening in August he killed a deer and laid it on top of the cabin to cool. That night three bears came for the deer. Frank was asleep in the cabin with the door open when the bears came and they came on in. He grabbed his gun but knew that it would not do to shoot, as the bears would be sure to get him. He ran out without his clothes on and waited on top of a high fence until the bears came out. Then he slipped into the cabin and lit a match to see that the bears were all gone. He fastened the door, but he thought the bears would tear the cabin down before they got the deer.

We asked him to tell us how he got away from the Indians four years before when they had him surrounded just above the Duck ranch, where Tom Shaw lives now. He said it was just about sundown and he had just moved to the place and as the place was new to the horses he tied them up at night so he would not have to look for them in the morning. He had just tied them up when he saw the Indians coming. He got his gun and all of his ammunition and ran for the brush. The Indians saw him, surrounded the brush and started to look for him. He laid as close to the ground as he could and one Indian crawled to within forty feet of him. The Indian saw him and shot at him, the ball grazing his side. The Indian thought he had killed Frank and crawled out. The horses were on the other side of Frank and toward the sunset, but the light in the west showed plain enough that he could see an Indian crawling toward the horses. When he got to the horse that was tied he raised up and said "How." Frank raised up on one elbow and gave the Indian a load of buckshot. He dropped and gave up the ghost. In a few minutes Frank saw the smoke begin to rise and knew that they had set the grass on fire and that would be the last of him. He determined to do the best he could. They had set fire all around the brush and when it had gotten close to him he grabbed his gun and ran across the burning grass, jumped into a small creek and ran as fast as he could. They never fired a shot at him. Then he went to a dugout where he had lived and where he had some potatoes. In traveling at night he had fallen off a rock and almost broke his leg, so he had to stay in the dugout until he was able to walk again. Then he started to the Swan ranch on the Sybille,[31] about forty miles away. One night he saw a man coming toward him. He hid but whistled, and the man answered him. It was Rube Rhoads, who told him how the Indians had killed many cowboys and stolen lots of horses.

The next morning we went hunting for elk. Tom and I were together and Teschemacher and de Billier. When we left the ranch we had to leave some guns there and that made us short on guns and ammunition, so I had to take what was left and that was an old army gun. Tom and I went down a small creek for a few miles until we came to a small mountain, then he went on the east side and I went on the west

73

side. I looked up the mountain after I had gone a mile or so and at the top I saw a big bull elk looking at me. The mountains, the elk, the gun and the ammunition were all new to me and I thought the elk was only a short distance away. I think now that he must have been a quarter of a mile away. I shot at him and as he never moved I shot again, but that did not move him. I got the old pony and climbed the mountain. The shots had alarmed the elk and they were moving west and going not far from where I had been shooting. It was a pleasing sight to see them traveling. There were about 75 of them and the young ones were about a half mile behind, playing and grazing at their leisure. They were then over a mile from me and I thought that if ever I was going to get an elk out of that bunch I would have to hustle. I looked the country over and could see that they were making for some hills about seven miles away. I got off the mountain and went up a small creek that hid me from the elk until I got ahead of them, keeping out of sight all the time until I got to the hills. I rode to the top of the hill and dropped the reins, letting the pony graze while I crawled down the hill. The elk came along leisurely directly toward me. When they got within half a mile of me they started to run. I had heard hunters say that if there was a large bunch of them to shoot ahead of them and they would bunch up. This I did and they bunched up. I had about a hatful of cartridges and I poured them out on the ground and began to shoot, snapping about half the time. I could not judge the

74

distance all at once. The elk started to run and a large cow was leading the bunch. I drew down on her elevating the old gun above her.

I broke her neck and when she dropped the others rounded up again. Then I learned that I had been shooting only at their feet and legs, but I did not stop firing until I had exploded the last cartridge. When I got up to go to my horse the elk started again and as they ran past me I could see that I had broken a number of legs. They ran up a creek. I was on level ground until I got ahead of them. Then I dropped down on the creek and the bunch hurried up until they all went past me. Just about this time I was very much excited. There were ten big bulls, with large horns. After the first ones passed me the others would not change their course. I was going as fast as the old horse would go, which was not very fast. As the crippled ones would come up I would fall in ahead of them and they would either turn out of the bunch or stop to fight.

I had turned out about four head of them with legs broken, when a nice young cow stopped to fight. By this time the old pony was out of wind and my pulse was up to fever heat. I jumped down and the elk came for me. The horned ones fight like cattle with their horns and are very vicious, but the cows have no horns and rear high in the air and lunge at you, butting like a goat. This cow reared and as she came at me I hit her with the gun on the head and the barrel went one way and the stock in another. The blow seemed to have no effect on the elk. As she came at me again I dodged to one side and caught her around the neck. She hit one foot on my chest and sent me about fifteen feet down the hill. Before I could get on my feet she lit on me, biting and stomping me. I caught her around the neck and by this time I had my butcher knife and she was so close to me that she could only reach my coat pocket. I never stopped cutting until I could feel the blood running and then she started to run. She was going so fast that I had to let loose, but she only went about a hundred yards until she dropped. This was one of my proudest moments. I had killed one of the large game animals of the Northwest.

We were then on the Laramie Plains and the wind had blown the snow off in spots, in other places it was 20 inches deep. I went back on the trail until I saw another crippled one had turned off and I had to follow it for a mile or two before I came up with a large cow that was lying down in a draw. She could not run, but started to fight. When they fight they made a loud, sharp noise, such as I never heard any other animal make, and she started this noise and came for me. I had nothing to fight with but the knife. The elk had a front foot shot off. I got on a bank about ten feet high, secured a rock that weighed about twelve pounds and as the cow came at me I threw the rock with both hands and hit her in the head. This only stopped her for a moment. I ran and jumped on the pony and as I went into the saddle she made a lunge at me and went over the pony. As she made the jump the pony sprang back and she missed me. She then was very sick from the shot and the lick in the head, so she lay down and began to groan and roll in the deep snow. I slipped up and tried to hold her down stabbing her once, but she got up. I ran to the stump of a large tree and she ran me around it several times and then lay down again. This time I never let her get up.

I then went back to the trail and saw another track going off to the hills. I followed this for about two miles and found another elk, a yearling bull with his first year's horns and a hind foot broken. He ran and I followed a short distance until he stopped to fight. He came for me and I dodged. The next time he came I dodged and caught him by one horn. He fought fast and furious and got me down, but I kept his hoofs out of my face until I could get one lick at his throat with the knife. As the blood started to run good, and all over me, he started to run. I let go and he ran over me, but he only went a short distance until he dropped.

Then it was sundown and only a short distance from where I had done the shooting. I went back to where I had broken the cow's neck and dressed her as I had the others. It was then dark and I was about ten miles from camp. The old pony was about all in, but it was a bright, moonlight night and I had watched the hills all day and they were all covered with snow and you could see them for miles. When I got back within five miles of camp I came to the creek we were camped on and I knew that the camp was up the creek. I could not tell which way the water was running until I had broken the ice and put my hand in the water to determine which way it was flowing.

About this time I heard a gun shot and I knew where the camp was. They thought that I was lost and were shooting to call me in. I was so sick I could hardly sit on my horse. The hand to hand battles had been too much for me. When I got in I had a hard time to make the fellows believe that I had done anything except get lost, but when they looked at my hands and saw my clothes they asked me how many I had killed. I told them four and Teschemacher ran up and patted me on the back and said: "Good boy, Jim. We will go home tomorrow. Won't we, Jim?" I got some hot coffee and felt better and after washing rolled into bed.

DeBillier had killed an elk that day. It took us all the next day to gather up the ones I had killed and early the following day we started for home, arriving at the ranch that night. We had good quarters and a good cook there. We then had meat enough to last until Spring.

I arrived on the Laramie River in September, 1879, and found Billy Bacon, who then owned the road ranch at Uva and knew most every man in Wyoming who owned cattle as far north as the Cheyenne River. F. M. Phillips, five miles down the river, owned the h outfit and Joe Morris was his foreman. Up the North Laramie was the F outfit, owned by T. A. Kent, with about 8,000 head of cattle. Eight miles up the North Laramie was the I-H outfit, owned by Heck Reel, with about 7,000 head of cattle. On the head of Cottonwood creek was located the Duck outfit, owned by the Warner Brothers, Will and Howard, with about 3,000 head. Ben Johnson and John Jones were on upper Horseshoe, as also were Macfarlane and Jim Reeder, all of whom had about 1,000 head. Johnson and Walker on lower Horseshoe, had several thousand head of cattle, but had commenced to move them to the Cheyenne River in 1879. Bob Bruster owned 2,500 head on the North Laramie, but moved them out in 1879. That was about all of the cattle in this country then, until you got up on the LaBonte.[32]

On the LaBonte the Guthries and Douglas Willow owned lots of cattle and over on the LaPrele were Joe Kennedy, George Cross, Dennis Leman, Hod Emerson and the Bakers owned many head. Clint Graham, who owned the old 66 ranch, called Riverview now, had moved out and gone to Montana.[33]

In January, 1880, Teschemacher & de Billier bought out the Warners on Cottonwood. I had been on the Duck ranch most of the winter and had managed with a little help to kill game enough to furnish the outfit with fresh meat. There were plenty of white and blacktail deer and elk and a few buffalo. John Reese was then foreman for the company, the company consisting of Arthur and Hubert Teschemacher and Fred de Billier.[34] The cash on hand was $40,000.

On the 3rd day of February, 1880, John Reese came to me and asked if I would like to work for the company. I said that I had been promised a job by the Warners to go west in the spring and bring a herd of cattle through from Oregon.[35] John laughed and said they would have no money, but I told him that Warners had asked me in case they did not drive to go to the head of Belle Fourche River and build them a ranch, but John advised me to have nothing to do with them. So on that day I started to work for the new company at $30 a month, with the promise of a raise as the company grew up. I still continued to hunt most of the time, but as the Boston bloods lived on the ranch the foreman had to appear as though he was busy.

A year later the company founded a ranch on Cottonwood, 600 head of cattle and a few horses. Then business commenced to pick up. The owners asked me and my brother, Tom, to go down and run the road ranch. I had to go at once to represent the company, but they kept the cook. Tobe Miller had run a saloon, but in the deed the company had stipulated that he was to dispose of all of the stuff in the saloon, as it did not want any of that stuff left on the ranch. Miller had about 200 bottles of beer and many bottles of whiskey, which he sold to anybody who wanted it. The men came for it later, but I was not in any of Miller's deals, all the trades being left to the cook, who was aching for Miller to get away so he could do as he wished with the liquor.

I think the cook managed to hold out lots of beer, for when other men who had road ranches came for the stuff he told them that Miller had left the bar and fixtures, but had taken most of the stock of liquor and pulled out for Colorado. The cook would set out about four bottles of beer a day and would hand me one. I had never drank any bottled beer, but as he was insistent I tried to drink one. It seemed to give me fever and I never tried any more. One night a bunch of cowboys came to stay all night and after supper started playing cards and drinking. The cook had told me and others that in Denver he posed as a fighting man and had been in the boxing ring for years. This night, when I thought it was time to go to bed, I told them so, but the cook insisted that he was "it" at the ranch and we had some words. I started to go to my room and he thought I was going after my gun. He ran after me and stepped between me and the door and said: "Now, let's not have any trouble." I told him if he would get out and take the beer and whiskey with him we would not have any trouble.

Tom then came from the other ranch and started in to run a road ranch hotel. Somehow we got along with it until they could send a man and woman from Cheyenne. In the spring after we had had our horse roundup and got the horses together we found there were some bad actors in the bunch. The boss told Tom and I that we must ride them all out. The first one that I got was not a bad horse, but had learned a few bad tricks. As I started to get into the saddle he turned under me and let me down on my head on the other side and ran off with my saddle. There were men there to watch the fun and they ran him back, everyone thinking that he must be a bad one. I had learned when a boy to hobble my stirrups and when the horse was being brought back I slipped a small piece of rope into my pocket and when fixing the saddle slipped the rope under the horse and tied my stirrups. The horse bucked good, I waved my hat in the air and got the reputation of being a fine rider.

In the spring in sending out the "reps," as the men were called who represented a company or a brand, I was sent with the F. M. Phillips outfit, which was to go down to the Sidney bridge on the North Platte River and there meet the southern roundup, that would work down the North Platte to North Platte City, then work the South Platte River through Colorado. The northern roundup was to work the North Platte River and all of its tributaries up to Fort Laramie, and there meet the Billy Irvine roundup, which was working the north side of the river and would there cross over and work the south side of the river to Deer Creek, above Fort Fetterman.[36]

The meeting at Sidney bridge was the biggest thing I ever saw in the way of a roundup. Everyone seemed to get there on time and on the morning of the 25th of May, 1880, the work commenced. There were 150 men and over 1,200 head of work and saddle horses. Everyone was represented and most of the old-time cowboys were there. There were Gunnysack Pete, Woodbox Jim, Driftwood Bill and Tobacker Jake. There were eighteen outfits represented. The two roundups started, Billy Larkins to run the roundup. Some say that Mr. Larkins made the mistake of putting all the cattle in one bunch and I tell you it took a good cowboy to get his cattle.

The two roundups worked together the first day. All the country along the river for miles was level and there were lots of cattle, for we must have rounded up between five and six thousand head, which were thrown together in one bunch. Mr. Larkins asked an old cow man by the name of Cy Doty, who ran an outfit for Black Tom Swan, if he knew the country to the west and if he was familiar with a certain large basin. Doty said he did. He was then instructed by Larkins to take fifty men, go to the head of the creek that ran through the basin and drive it clean.[37]

It was the way in those days for the man who was sent to make the drive to be business-like and start out very fast and ride that way for a mile or so. We went to the head of the large basin, where there were about 1,000 head of cattle and it was a grand sight to see this crew of men go around this bunch of cattle. The cattle in these days would be driven from Texas, a hundred thousand head each year, and the cattlemen would go to Ogallala to receive them. Ogallala, on the Union Pacific, was the one point they all made from southern Texas and the cattle would be purchased and turned loose on the fine range to winter. The next year they would be wild, so the cowboys would have to ride fast to turn them. The other hundred men went down the river toward Ash Hollow. I got on top of a hill, from where I saw the men go round the big basin in a hard run for ten miles and all the cattle moving in a hard run. To the east we could see the hundred men going in a hard run and about 5,000 head of cattle doing their best to get away.

This hundred men in a hard gallop looked very much like a troop of soldiers after Indians. About 11 o'clock we got about 5,000 head in one bunch and then was when the fun began. Everybody seemed to be in a hurry and wanted to cut cattle. One little Texas steer would not be cut out and the cowboys rode him until he was tired. Five or six boys had their ropes swinging, but they could not catch the steer, as he would have his horns under a cow or a horse. This seemed to amuse a big Englishman very much, as he had never before seen a man rope a cow. He followed around for awhile and then jumped off his horse, caught the steer by the tail and yelled with all his might: "Come on, boys, I've got him. Bring on your ropes and I'll put them all on him." By this time the boys had all the fun they wanted and rode away, as the man who owned the steer had lost all interest in him. The steer dragged the big Englishman into the roundup and in a few seconds he was surrounded by big, wild longhorns, that had been driven from Corpus Christi or somewhere along the Gulf of Mexico the year before. Big as he was, the

Englishman had to resort to his six-shooter to get out.

The next morning we separated and the Wyoming men, seven outfits, started up the river, while the southern men started with eight or nine wagons, or outfits, down the river. It was quite a sight to see those two big roundups, one going north, the other south. We stopped the second day at the Coad ranch, belonging to Mark and John Coad, who owned the C-12 outfit, with lots of cattle. They afterwards sold out for $750,000.[38] We worked on up the river by Courthouse Rock, a very large rock that resembled the usual courthouse, standing about 150 feet high out on the open prairie.

The next big ranch was the Crotan ranch, or half-circle-block, on Jumping creek. It was later sold for a million dollars. Then came the old Bridle Bit, owned by Sturgis & Lane. The ranch house was formerly a stage station, built by Cuny & Ecoffey, who ran a stage line from Julesburg, on the Union Pacific, to Virginia City, Mont. It was built of sod. The barn, corral and outhouses were also built of sod and at that time were in good condition, with loopholes all around the house, where the men could shoot out when the enemy came. We were then at the mouth of Horse Creek, and we worked that creek to the state road, and all of Goshen Hole, Fox, Box Elder and Cherry Creeks. We had rather a stormy day when we pulled from Cherry to Box Elder Creek. We had had little moisture that year, but on this morning it was snowing and very cold.

The captain ordered us to move to Box Elder. We then moved back to Fort Laramie, where we met the W. C. Irvine roundup and Zach Thomason, range manager for the Swan Land and Cattle Company, with a big outfit. Five wagons pulled back from Fort Laramie, but others joined us and we worked up the Laramie River, then the Sybille and on around until we were in sight of Laramie City.[39]

Then we came back around Ragged Top mountain and down Crow creek, camping on that creek five miles below Cheyenne. When we got around in the hills we met two more outfits and some very nice fellows, including Tom Babbitt, John McLaughlin, Dan Arnold and Billie Lannen.[40] For several miles we had nothing to do and we went to Cheyenne very fast. Some of the Laramie Plains men were a long ways ahead of us and had gotten a lot of ladies' gowns, hats, shoes and stockings and were galloping over town, with all the policemen after them. It was rather exciting, as the police and cowboys exchanged shots; but the cowboys got out of town, went to their camps, changed horses and threw away the women's clothes and the police did not know them any more.

We rounded up Crow creek to the old Campstool ranch, then back to the head of Lone Tree Creek, Windy Hollow and south to Jack Springs in Colorado. We made one roundup south and west of Jack Springs and got into the farming country and the farmers came out on the fight, as they thought we were driving through and taking their cattle. About twenty of them came out when we had rounded up.

JAMES C. SHAW, 1882
From an original photograph taken by Kirkwood in Cheyenne, Wyoming

They rode in and started cutting out their cattle. Most of them were in the fields at work when the alarm was sounded and did not take the trouble to remove the chain harness from their horses. It made the cattle wild to see the fellows chasing through the roundup, riding bareback and blind bridle, and with the harness chains rattling, and it kept the cowboys busy to hold the cows in the country until the roundup foreman could cut some of them out. One fellow, riding a mule bareback, came out to the herd whooping and cursing, and the mule did not want to go alone and ran to every horse he saw. The man seemed to be in a great hurry and we asked him where he was going. He said he was going home to get a pitchfork to cut out his cows with.

We finished the roundup there and the next morning we were to go for our homes, three wagons for the Laramie Plains and two wagons for the Laramie River. There was a big event to be settled. A footrace had been arranged and was to be run at the end of the roundup. As the last of the cattle had been cut out and the farmers had their animals, one of the farmers came to a cattleman named Frank Hubbs and said he had some yearlings he wished to sell. Frank went and looked them over and said the yearlings had been strained. The farmer was puzzled and asked how. Frank said their stomachs had been burnt out on hot milk.

The different outfits had bet about $300 a side on the foot race, which was to be run just as we were about to start and the drivers on their seats waiting to crack the whip. Wes Price and Fred Gibbon were the racers. A big, black negro named John Price was a cook for one of the Plains outfit and just as the men were ready to start he came out and looked over the runners, saying: "Well, dat do settle it. If dat don't beat all. Look here, Mr. Price, if you don't beat dat fellow you aint kin to me no moh." Wes Price won the race. Twenty-five years later Wes Price came to Douglas and lived there many years and was a very good citizen.

The Laramie Plains men went to their ranches on the Plains and we started for the Laramie River and the Swan outfit for their range on the Sybille and many other creeks. Zach Thomason was then the range manager for the Swan company and I don't think a better man could have been selected. His salary was $3,600 a year. Dan Swan was running the wagon that represented the Swan company from our country. I cut loose from him at the Seven Keg Muleshoe ranch on the Sybille and made it across the Laramie River, driving my horses and cattle, with two men to help me.[41]

The next year I ran the Duck Bar outfit and the state laid out the roundups, assigning me to round-up No. 5, which was to begin at Fort Laramie and work all of the country between Fort Laramie and the range of Black Hills on the west and the Platte river to Fort Fetterman.[42]

NOTES

[1] For the classic account of Abilene, Kansas, during the cattle trailing heyday beginning in 1867, see Joseph G. McCoy, *Historic Sketches of the Cattle Trade of the West and Southwest*. Ramsey, Millett & Hudson, Kansas City, Missouri, 1874.

[2] By 1875 cattle raising in New Mexico had become the second largest industry (sheep raising being first) in the territory. Principal markets for the cattlemen were the numerous army posts, the Indian distribution program, the burgeoning mining areas in the Colorado and northern New Mexico Rockies, the rapidly expanding ranching industry in Wyoming, and the railroad construction camps in Colorado and Kansas. Some New Mexico herds were trailed to the Kansas railroad shipping points for shipment to Kansas City and Chicago. Large cattle operations were located along the Pecos and Red Rivers, as well as the Rio Grande Valley. Loving and Goodnight had pioneered the transfer of Texas stock to New Mexico, but the Spanish settlers had founded the New Mexico herds beginning in 1598 and in the following centuries had made the territory an outstanding stock raising region. Herbert O. Brayer, "Cattle in New Mexico," *American Cattle Producer*, June 1945, 8 *et seq.*

[3] New Mexico in the 'seventies was in a tumultuous condition. The forceable blending of Hispanic, Anglo-American, and Indian cultures produced various degrees of economic, social and political chaos. Frontier conditions of law and order prevailed. In the cattle industry a well organized rustler group, made up of Indians and New Mexicans, stole thousands of head of Texas cattle and drove them across the plains to the New Mexico ranches. J. Evetts Haley, "The Comanchero Trade," *The Southwestern Historical Quarterly* (Austin, Texas), XXXVIII, 157 ff.

[4] Colonel Albert G. Boyce became one of the great cattlemen of the Southwest. He drove a trail herd from Texas to California in 1867 and then became a partner of and trail boss for the famous Snyder

brothers, driving some 25,000 head of cattle up the trail from Texas to Julesburg, Colorado, in 1877. In subsequent years he was a familiar figure on the trails and ranges of the West, and, in 1887, he became manager of the 3,000,000 acre XIT Ranch with operations stretching from the home ranch in west Texas to the maturing ranges in Montana. James Cox, *Historical and Biographical Record of the Cattle Industry of the Cattlemen of Texas and Adjacent Territory* (St. Louis, 1895), 494-495.

Dudley H. and John W. Snyder of Georgetown, Texas — along with their brother Tom Snyder — were among the largest and most active of the Texas cattlemen during the range cattle era. Tens of thousands of Longhorn cattle carrying their brand made the drive north to Kansas, Nebraska, Dakota, Wyoming and Montana, and many famous cattlemen had their start with Snyder herds. Both brothers were trustees of the estate of Colorado's pioneer cattleman, John Iliff, and directed the liquidation of his large cattle "empire". They were among the founders of the Wyoming Stock Growers Association in 1874 and Dudley Snyder served on its executive board. By the mid-'eighties the Snyders were running cattle in Texas, Colorado, Wyoming and Montana, and their trail herds were also known in Kansas, Nebraska, the Dakotas and the Indian Territory.

[5] Lee Moore was also one of the Snyder brothers trail men. His colorful autobiographical story, written in 1915, is printed in *Letters from Old Friends and Members of the Wyoming Stock Growers Association* (Cheyenne, Wyoming, 1923), 33-41. (Hereinafter cited as *Letters*.)

[6] For Tom Shaw's account see Virginia Cole Trenholm, *Footprints on the Frontier* (Douglas, Wyoming, 1945), 133 *et seq.* "Hi" Webb was the noted cattleman and Chisholm Trail drover, A. H. Webb, who later became one of the founders of the Wyoming Stock Growers Association and a partner of Charles F. Coffee. They founded a ranch on Box Elder Creek, sixty-five miles north of Cheyenne in 1873. Charles F. Coffee, *Letters*, 27.

[7] Arthur Coffee had come up the trail from Texas in the 'seventies. He soon had his own ranch and became one of the first to change from Texas Longhorn cattle to the bulkier and more profitable Oregon or "American" cattle.

[8] Howard and Will Warner were also former Texas cattlemen who came up the trail with a Longhorn herd and founded the Duck ranch on Cottonwood Creek in Wyoming. They were also among

90

the first cattlemen to stock their ranch with the heavier Oregon stock.

[9] Fort Griffin was on the famed *Western* or *Fort Griffin and Dodge City Trail* pioneered in 1876 by D. S. Combs with a herd belonging to Ellison and Dewees. From Dodge City a new trail, the *Northern Trail,* was opened to Ogallala, Pine Bluffs, the Chugwater, Powder River, the Black Hills and Montana. Garnet M. and Herbert O. Brayer, *America's Cattle Trails* (American Pioneer Trails Association, 1952), 62.

[10] Ogallala became the "cattle capital" of Nebraska. Texas trail herds bound for Dakota, Wyoming and Montana stopped here before crossing the Platte. For a decade tens of thousands of Wyoming, Dakota, and even Montana cattle were driven to the stock yards along the Union Pacific Railroad and loaded into cars for eastern markets. For a short period in the late 'seventies and early 'eighties thousands of cattle trailed eastward from Oregon were also loaded and shipped from the Ogallala yards.

[11] By accident Jim Shaw had joined up with one of the largest trail contracting outfits operating out of Texas, Ellison and Sherrill, owned and operated by two noted cattlemen, James H. Sherrill and James F. Ellison. Richard "Dick" Withers, trail boss for Ellison & Sherrill, was in charge of the drive of 5500 head (Shaw noted only 4800) of Longhorns, "the largest herd ever seen on the trail." His own account of this drive may be read in J. Marvin Hunter, *The Trail Drivers of Texas* (Cokesbury Press, Nashville, Tenn., 1925), 311-313. Withers later became a successful rancher at Boyes, Montana. George Lyons had first come up the trail in 1870 with 1500 cattle from south Texas to Dodge City via Doan's Store. (Hunter, *ibid.,* 534.) William J. Jackman, who was also a "top hand" and trail boss, became a successful rancher and also wrote an account of this drive. (Hunter, *ibid.,* 856-861.)

Trail crews were thoroughly organized and each man assigned a definite position along the herd at which he rode daily. The two riders at the head or "point" of the strung-out herd were called "pointers", "point riders", or "point men." On opposite sides of the long, thin line of cattle, from a quarter to a third of the way back from the point, rode the "swings" whose job it was to see that the beasts kept up the pace and stayed in position. Another third of the way back rode the "flanks" or "flank men" who kept the herd moving, prevented straggling, and watched that the herd didn't break into two divisions. At the rear rode the "drags" whose difficult, and dirty job it was to keep slow, lazy, lame or perverse animals moving forward.

[12] "F.F.V.'s" — First Families of Virginia.

[13] Prairie Dogs have been eaten for centuries by the Indians of the Southwest; these small herbivorous animals — which weigh as much as three or four pounds on occasion — taste somewhat like a prairie rabbit.

[14] Woods referred to a not unusual incident in which part of the thirsty herd broke away when water was scented. Such accidents were dangerous to both men and beasts and usually brought about a sharp reprimand from the trail boss. It was also considered a blot on the record of the cowboy responsible for the break, although in many instances the men could not have prevented the division. Woods obviously refused to accept responsibility for the break recounted by Jim Shaw.

[15] Alkaline water was and is very common throughout the Southwest. Thirsty men and beasts who ignored the brackish taste frequently experienced serious attacks of diarrhea, dysentery and even unconsciousness. Certain forms of alkalinity resulted in death to both the riders and their cattle, and more often to sheep. Relief was gained in many ways. Charles Goodnight reported that a tea made of bachelor's button or snakeroot was effective. Trail cooks, who also served as doctor and nurse for the crews, favored a flour and water batter as salty as the patient could drink. For flour, which was often scarce, the inside bark of the familiar cottonwood tree — which grew along most streams — was substituted and boiled into a strong tea. "It was a hell of a drink, a wonderful astringent, and a bitter dose. But it is a sure shot." J. Evetts Haley, *Charles Goodnight, Cowman and Plainsman* (Norman, 1949), 85. For other cures (including the unique "apply the white of an egg on the abdomen") see Frost Woodhull, "Ranch Remedios," *Man, Bird and Beast* (Publications of the Texas Folklore Society, volume VIII, Austin, 1930), 54.

[16] Even the alternately dusty and muddy, clap-board, boom-town of Dodge City could appear "a most beautiful little town" to a cowboy who had been riding "drag" on the lonely trail for a month or more. For an excellent picture of Dodge City during its heyday see Stanley Vestal, *Queen of Cowtowns, Dodge City . . . 1872-1886,* Harpers, 1952.

[17] *Adobe*, or "dobie", as it is commonly called, buildings were constructed of sun baked bricks made out of prairie mud mixed with straw or other binding material. When hardened and properly laid, these bricks made excellent and long lasting building material with outstanding insulation properties.

[18] The famous Wyatt Earp was assistant town marshall in 1879.

[19] For a good description of Ogallala during the trail herd era see John Bratt, *Trails of Yesterday* (The University Publishing Company, Lincoln, Neb., 1921), 245-247.

[20] Richard G. "Dick" Head was another of the Texas trail cattlemen to acquire fame throughout the range country. He began as a thirty dollar a month cowboy and became trail manager for Colonel John J. Myers. For seven years he "pushed" herds to Abilene, Wichita, Great Bend, Ellsworth, and Dodge City in Kansas, and to Indian agencies, military posts and ranches in Wyoming, the Black Hills, Utah, Nevada and California. T. Marvin Hunter, *The Trail Drivers of Texas* (Cokesbury Press, Nashville, Tenn, 1925), 734-736.

[21] Captain Edgar B. Bronson, later a noted author, used a seagull brand and had his range at the head of White River and the Upper Niabrara in Nebraska. Frank C. Bosler was a native of Cumberland County, Pennsylvania. With his brother he founded a ranch on Blue Creek, north of Ogallala, and engaged in the cattle business in Nebraska, Dakota, and in Wyoming. In the latter he was incorporator and trustee of the Iron Mountain Ranch Company. His most successful operations, however, were in Nebraska. At various times he was a partner or stockholder in cattle operations organized by Alexander H. Swan and Francis E. Warren.

[22] Francis E. Warren was born in Hinsdale, Mass., in 1844. Following his army service in the Civil War he went to Cheyenne and took charge of the A. R. Converse store. While still in the mercantile business he established, in 1873, the Warren Livestock Company which became one of the largest sheep and cattle ranches in the West. His livestock operations spread to Colorado, Dakota and Nebraska. Warren was active in the Wyoming Stock Growers Association and served as both territorial and state governor of Wyoming, as well as United States senator from 1890-1893, 1895-1929. From 1878 to 1880 Warren was partner in several cattle raising operations in Wyoming and Dakota with William Guiterman. The latter owned a ranch on the Belle Fourche and another on Hat Creek and the Cheyenne River.

[23] Fort Robinson was in the northwest corner of Nebraska.

[24] By "wrestle" Shaw referred to the job of throwing the animal off its feet and on its side after it had been roped and before it was branded.

[25] Camp Sheridan was an army post in northern Nebraska founded to prevent Indian depredations and white transgressions on the reservations.

[26] Alexander H. Swan was born in Greene County, Pennsylvania, in 1831. After a successful venture in raising Hereford cattle in Indianola, Iowa, he moved to Wyoming in 1872. With his brother Tom he purchased the John Spark's herd on the Chugwater and thereby laid the foundation for the Swan cattle "empire", the largest in Wyoming during the 'eighties. From 1879 to 1885 they owned or controlled a purported 200,000 head of cattle. Hubert Howe Bancroft, *History of Nevada, Colorado, & Wyoming* (San Francisco, 1890), 800. Alexander Swan was incorporator, trustee and general manager of Swan Brothers, the National Cattle Company, Swan & Frank Live Stock Company, Swan, Frank & Anthony Cattle Company, Hillsdale Land & Cattle Company, Swan Land & Cattle Company Ltd., the Wyoming Hereford Association and many others.

[27] See Trenholm, *op. cit.*, 133 *et seq.*

[28] A. H. "Heck" Reel (1837-1900) was born in Jacksonville, Illinois, and went to Colorado in 1860 during the Pikes Peak Gold Rush. He moved to Wyoming, became a successful freighter, and was elected a member of the Cheyenne City Council in 1869. He became mayor of Cheyenne, one of the founders of the Wyoming Stock Growers Association, a member of the territorial and state legislature (both as representative and senator), and successful cattleman. His "seventy-six" ranch was on the Medicine Bow and his "ninety-six" ranch spread to the Ham's Fork, Pomeroy Basin, Dutch George Basin, the Muddy, the Fontenelle, La Barge and Green River, and in Uinta County. For a Shaw story concerning Reel's foreman, Sylvester Sherman, see footnote 43.

[29] Frederick O. deBillier was of French descent. He came to Wyoming from New York and went into the cattle business with Hubert E. Teschemacher, a native of Massachusetts, graduate of Harvard University and man of considerable means. Both men came to Wyoming in 1879 and founded the Teschemacher & deBillier Cattle Company which also included Arthur Teschemacher and Theodore Roosevelt. Their range was at Bridger's Ferry on the North Platte and on the Bitter, Cottonwood and Wagon Hound. Here, on their famous Duck Bar ranch (purchased largely from the Warner brothers, see footnote #8), they ran about 25,000 head of cattle. Teschemacher was secretary and trustee of the John Hunton Co., the Riverside Land & Cattle Co., and took an active part in the affairs of the stock growers association. He served in both houses of the territorial legislature and was a member of the constitutional convention. The hard winter of 1886-1887

94

hit the Duck Bar herds seriously, but it was the active participation of both owners in the Johnson County War in 1892 — with the "Invaders" — which caused them to liquidate their cattle ranches in 1893. They *gave* two of their ranches to James C. Shaw and Tom Shaw and sold their remaining cattle to Francis E. Warren for $15.00 a head. DeBillier died in France in 1933 and Teschemacher in Boston in 1906.

[30] Frank Preager was a German Swiss who came to Colorado with his parents in the gold rush of 1859. The family settled on the Big Thompson and Preager went to Wyoming in 1872 with a herd of 150 head of improved cattle. In 1875 he moved to the Cottonwood where he built his ranch only to have it destroyed within a few weeks by an Indian raiding party. He rebuilt the cabin and his ranch became a popular stopping place for cowboys.

[31] This was Alex Swan's Two Bar ranch just west of Hunton's place.

[32] William L. Bacon owned a road ranch in La Bonte Park near present Uva. In 1886 he killed Jack Saunders, co-operator of the "Hog Ranch" near Ft. Fetterman and a short while later was himself killed in a gun battle. Frank M. "Butcher" Phillips, who ran the "h" brand, had a ranch on the Laramie River at the mouth of the Chugwater where he ran several thousand head of Texas cattle. He purchased his initial cattle from Iliff in 1873, and sold out in 1885 to the Cheyenne mercantile house of Whipple & Hay. Thomas A. Kent, Cheyenne banker and cattleman, was a Philadelphian and incorporator of the T. A. Kent & Co., the Cheyenne Investment Company, and Lowe Cattle Company as well as one of the co-founders of the Wyoming Stock Growers Association in 1873-1874. Relative to the Warners see footnote #8. William F. Macfarlane of Uva had the 14 brand on the Horseshoe. Using the 45 brand, James R. Reeder of Uva also ran his cattle on the Horseshoe. Robert Walker and Skew Johnson, veterans of the Confederate army, established the first ranch on the Horseshoe in 1874 with 3000 Texas Longhorn cattle. They were attacked by Indians in 1875 and 1876 and lost several cowboys, but saved most of their herd.

[33] William E. and S. A. Guthrie of Albany and Converse Counties were members of the Wyoming Stock Growers Association beginning in 1879 and 1880. Will Guthrie was assistant roundup foreman of district four in 1881. He served on the association's executive committee from 1886 to 1900, and was a member of the last Wyoming territorial legislature. Both brothers were incorporators of the Guthrie & Oscamp Cattle Co., which used the spearhead brand and ranged on La Bonte, Wagon Hound and La Prele

Creeks. Will Guthrie took an active part in the Johnson County War and afterward lived in Nebraska. In 1926 he wrote an interesting article for the *Annals of Wyoming* (V, No. 1, 26-31) entitled "The Open Range Cattle Business in Wyoming."

Joseph H. Kennedy ran the UH outfit on La Prele Creek and the Upper Box Elder in Albany County. He was roundup foreman of district #5 in 1882 and a member of the Wyoming Stock Growers Association executive committee in 1896. State Senator George H. Cross was a native of Canada (1854) who went to Colorado in 1875 and moved to Wyoming in 1877. He founded the VC ranch between the La Bonte and La Prele Creeks and was active in both county politics and the stock growers association. Hod Emerson was one of the firm of Emerson Brothers from Livermore, Colorado, who ran a ranch on La Prele Creek, the Upper Box Elder, and the Bed Tick near Fort Fetterman. E. L. Baker also had a small spread on the La Prele where he branded the quarter-circle diamond brand. Clint Graham drove cattle from Colorado and settled on La Bonte Creek in 1875.

34 John H. Rees (Reese) was on "Heck" Reel's HR Ranch in 1877 and in 1879 was foreman of Warner's Duck ranch. He was employed as an inspector for the stock growers association at Cheyenne from 1882 to 1888, and at Omaha from 1900 to 1901. Relative to the Teschemachers and Frederick O. de Billier see footnote #29.

35 Oregon cattle became the favorite base stock for many Wyoming ranches during the late 'seventies and early 'eighties when railroads made the leaner and more fractious Longhorns obsolete. For an account of this spectacular eastward movement of cattle from Oregon see J. Orin Oliphant, "The Eastward Movement of Cattle from the Oregon Country," *Agricultural History*, II, No. 1, 19 *et seq.*

36 See footnote #32 for F. M. Phillips. William C. "Billy" Irvine (1852-1924) was born in Pennsylvania and emigrated to Kansas in 1872 where he wintered a herd near Ogallala. In Nebraska in 1872 he formed a partnership with the Bosler Brothers (see footnote #21) of Pennsylvania, where he acquired the reputation for being an excellent cowman, "fighter and hot head." (Bratt, *op.cit.*, 245.) In the same year he went to Wyoming with the Ogallala Cattle Company and became one of the founders of the stock growers association. From Texas in 1876 he drove a trail herd of 4000 cattle to Wyoming, and in 1877 brought 3800 head more. He became associated with the Converse Cattle Company, served in the territorial legislature, was director of the Cheyenne Northern Railway and incorporator of numerous other companies. He held numerous

96

offices in the stock growers association and was its president from 1896 to 1911. Although his role in the Johnson County War cost him dearly, he recouped his fortunes and served with distinction in the state legislature and as state treasurer. In 1882 Irvine owned a ranch on Old Woman Creek.

[37] Thomas "Black Tom" Swan was a member of Swan Brothers and a stockholder in several other ranching companies. He was active in the stock growers association and a member of the territorial council in 1879.

[38] John F. and Mark M. Coad were primarily Nebraska ranchers with ranges at Scotts Bluff on the North Platte in Cheyenne County, and on Pumpkin Creek. John ran the Bar C cattle and Mark the "F Bar" or "F" brands. As a company the brothers used the Bar 12 brand. Both men were active members of the Wyoming Stock Growers Association from its organization in 1874.

[39] The Bridle Bit ranch was owned by Thomas Sturgis — second secretary of the stock growers association and prominent in territorial political life — and William C. Lane. The firm later became Sturgis, Lane & Goodall. The stage line was run by Adolph Cuny and Jules Ecoffey. The Swan manager, Zacharias Thomason, was one of the incorporators of Swan, Frank & Anthony Cattle Company, the Horse Creek Land & Cattle Company and the Ogallala Land & Cattle Company. He had his own ranch in 1883, the "o7", on the Laramie Plains and North Platte River.

[40] Albert T. "Tom" Babbitt was trustee, incorporator and general manager of the Standard Cattle Company. He was one of the most active supporters of the stock growers association and joint compiler of its first brand book issued in 1882. He served as president of the association in 1888-1889. In addition to his livestock business Babbitt was actively interested in the mineral development (copper especially) of Wyoming. Dan Arnold was assistant roundup foreman in 1887. William Lannen was roundup foreman of district #1 in 1883 and 1884, and assistant foreman in district #7 in 1885.

[41] Dan S. Swan was a member of the Swan Brothers company on Chugwater. He became a member of the stock growers association in 1875.

[42] Jim Shaw told many stories of his experiences in Wyoming, but, unfortunately, few were ever written down. In his "Indian Story of Sylvester Sherman," published in the *Annals of Wyoming* (III, No. 3, Jan. 1926), 177-180, he recalled another hunting incident in which some insight into his carefree life on the range can be found:

. . . I remember once he [Sylvester Sherman] saved my life by being a quick shot, and a man to think and to act quickly. I roped a bear, took a run on it and jerked it down, but as my saddle was not cinched up tight, I jerked it back on the horse's hip, but my rope was fastened under the saddle horn, so I could not throw it off. The rope had pulled me down on the side of the horse, the bear grabbed the rope in his front paws and began to pull the horse and I towards him, and all the time making a great noise. Just then Sherman came galloping up, and out with his six shooter and gave him a dead shot, but the noise had attracted the other bear in the brush, and it was coming for me, and the next instant he killed him too. This all happened in about five seconds, but it seemed hours to me. . . .

THE EDITORS are deeply indebted to Mr. Fred Rosenstock of Denver, Colorado, for the use of the autographed copy of Mr. Shaw's reminiscences, and to Mr. Everett Graff of Winnetka for the use of his library in preparation of the introduction and notes. Our appreciation is also due to Virginia Cole Trenholm for permission to quote from her *Footprints on the Frontier*, Douglas, Wyoming, 1945, and to James A. Shaw of Dubois, Wyoming and Kamloops, British Columbia, son of Tom Shaw and nephew of James C. Shaw. Mrs. Patti Shaw Gray and Clay D. Shaw of Orin, Wyoming, graciously supplied both pictures and information of material value.

Index

A

Abbot, "Teddy Blue", vii.
Abilene (Kan.), 13; 30; 89 fn.1; 93 fn.20.
Adair, John, v.
adobe, 47; 92 fn.17.
agent, Indian, 64; 65.
Agriculture History, 96 fn.35.
Albany County (Wyo.), 95-96 fn. 33.
Albert, Negro, 34; 36; 46; 47; 55.
Alfred, Negro, 19.
alkali, 43; 92 fn.15.
Alveno, —, 55.
American (Oregon) cattle, 90 fn.7.
American Cattle Producer, 89 fn.2.
American Cattle Trails, 91 fn.9.
American Pioneer Trails Ass'n, 91 fn.9.
ammunition, 14; 72; 73; 74; 75.
Annals of Wyoming, 96 fn.33; 97-98 fn.42.
antelope, 33; 60; 62; 67.
Army, U. S., 28; 40; 42; 52; 57; 58; 73; 84; 89 fn.2; post 93 fn.20.
Arnold, Dan, 86; 97 fn.40.
Ash Hollow, 84.
Austin (Tex.), 9; 14; 17; 25; 26; 51.
axle, wagon, 34.

B

Babbitt, Albert T., 86; 97 fn.40.
Bacon, William L. "Billy", 69; 78; 95 fn.32.
Baker, E. L., 96 fn.33.
Bancroft, Hubert Howe, 94 fn.26.
bankers, 95 fn.32.
Barker, Ben, 34; 55; 58-61; 65.
Barker, Cal, 23.
Barker, Nat, 23.
barrel, 16.
bears, 72; 98 fn.42.
bed packs, 14.
beef, v; 63; 65.
beer, 57; 80; 81.
Belgian horses, viii.
Bell County (Tex.), 9.
Belle Fourche, 80; 93 fn.22.
Belton (Tex.), 9.
Bennett, James, 26.
Bennett, Joe, 21.
Bennett, T. J., 12; 22; 23.
bible, 61.
Big Springs (Neb.), 56.
deBillier, Frederick O., v; vii; viii; 71; 73; 78; 79; 94-95 fn.29; 96 fn.34.
Billings County (Mont.), ix.
biscuits, 4; 31.
Black Hills (Dak.), 88; 91 fn.9; 93 fn.20.

P

Palmyra (Mo.), 2.
pass, Indian, 42.
pastures, vi.
Pennsylvania, 93 fn.21; 94 fn.26;
 96 fn.36.
Philadelphia, 95 fn.32.
Phillips, Frank M., 78; 82; 95
 fn.32; 96 fn.36.
Pierce, Mr., 55; 57-59.
pies, 68.
Pikes Peak Gold Rush, 94 fn.28;
 95 fn.30.
Pine Bluffs, 91 fn.9.
Pine Ridge Indian Reservation
 (Agency), vii, 61; 63-65.
Pioneering in Texas and Wyoming, xi.
pioneers, 26.
pistol, 10; 44-47; 51; 67.
pitchfork, 87.
plums, 50.
pocahontas, 38.
police, 48; Indian 64; 86.
Pomeroy Basin (Wyo.), 94 fn.28.
potatoes, 73.
powder, black, 10.
de Poysture, Jake, 55.
prairie, 85.
prairie dog, soup 38; 92 fn.13.
Preager, Frank, 71-72; 95 fn.30.
Price, John, 88.
Price, Wes, 88.
prices, ix; 4; 6; cattle 13; 22-23;
 54; 69; 85.

Q

quarrel, trail, 38-39; Dodge City
 48; Ogallala 51-52; 57; 59; 81.
*Queen of Cowtowns, Dodge City
 . . . 1872-1886*, 92 fn.16.
quicksand, 55.
quinine, 7.

R

rabbit, 38; 92 fn.13.
Ragged Top Mountain, 86.

railroads, viii; ix; 6; 9; 13; Union
 Pacific 51; 55; 68; 89 fn.2; 91
 fn.10; Cheyenne Northern
 Railway, 96 fn.36.
rain, xiii, 49.
"Ranch Remedios," 92 fn.15.
Ranches and ranching companies
 (see also under names of cattle-
 men and brands): v; vi; viii; xi;
 x; 28; 89 fn.2.
Bacon ranch, 69.
Bacon Rind ranch, ix.
Baker ranch, 79.
Bar C ranch, 97 fn.38.
Bar Circle ranch, 55.
Barker ranch, 23.
Bridle Bit ranch, 85; 97 fn.39.
Bob Bruster ranch, 79.
Camp Stool ranch, 86.
Coad Bros., "C-12" ranch, 85.
Comical Q, ix. See end sheet
 legend.
Converes Cattle Co., 96 fn.36.
Cottonwood ranch, 80.
George Cross ranch, 79.
Crotan "half-circle-block"
 ranch, 85.
Duck Bar ranch, vii; ix; x; 88;
 94-95 fn.29.
Duck ranch, 70; 72; 79; 90 fn.8;
 96 fn.34.
Emerson Bros. ranch, 79.
"F" ranch, 78.
"F Bar" ranch, 97 fn.38.
Clint Graham "66" ranch, 79.
Guthrie ranch, 79.
"h" ranch, 78.
HR ranch, vii; 69-70; 96 fn.34.
H3 ranch, 69.
"Hog Ranch," 95 fn.32.
Horse Creek Land & Cattle Co.,
 97 fn.39.
IH ranch, 78.
Iron Mountain Ranch Co., 93
 fn.21.
Skew Johnson ranch, 79.
John Jones ranch, 79.
J. H. Kennedy ranch, 79.

Shaw, John, 1; 12; 13.
Shaw, John Virgil, 2; 12; 13.
Shaw, Margaret Agnes, 2; 19.
Shaw, Mary Isabel, 2.
Shaw, Nancy, 2.
Shaw, Ninion, 2.
Shaw, Robert, 2.
Shaw, Sarah Evaline, 2; 20.
Shaw, Thomas Armstrong, vii; 2; 13-18; 26-27; 56; 69-73; 80-81; 90 fn.6; 94 fn.26; 95 fn.29.
Shaw, William J., 2.
sheep, 89 fn.2; 93 fn.22.
shell, terrapin, 62.
sheriffs, deputy, 46; 51-52.
Sherman, Sylvester, 70; 94 fn.28; 97-98 fn.42.
Sherrill, James H., 31; 35; 52; 53; 91 fn.11.
Shire horses, viii.
Shorthorn, cattle breed, viii.
shotgun, 26; 73.
Sidney (Neb.), bridge 82.
silver, 2.
Silver City (N.M.), viii.
slaves, 6; 16; 17.
smallpox, 15; 63.
Snively, Mr., 26.
snow, xiii; 71; 76; 77.
Snyder, Dudley H., 90 fn.4.
Snyder, John W., 90 fn.4.
Snyder, Tom, 90 fn.4.
soldiers, 28; 58; 84.
Somerset (Ky.), 1.
South, The, 24.
South Carolina, 69.
South Dakota, x; xiii; see also Dakota Territory.
The Southwestern Historical Quarterly, 89 fn.3.
Spanish, settlers, 89 fn.2.
Sparks, John, 94 fn.26.
speculators, cotton, 6.
spoon, 62.
stages, 17; station 85.
stampede, xiii; 37; 39-40; 46-47; 58; 59.
stealing, cattle, 13; 14; 17; 62.

Stetson, hat v.
Stevens, Prof. Isaac, 20.
Stiles, Mrs., 25.
stirrups, 82.
stock yards, 91 fn.10.
stores, 51; 64.
storms, 32; 33; 37; 71; 85.
strychnine, 11.
Sturgis, Henry, v.
Sturgis, Thomas, 97 fn.39.
Swan, Alex, v; 69; ranch 73; 93 fn.21; 94 fn.26; 95 fn.31.
Swan, Dan, v; 88; 97 fn.41.
Swan, Thomas "Black Tom", v; 83; 97 fn.37.
Swan, Thomas "Red Tom," v.
swearing, 60.
Swiss, German 95 fn.30.

T

Talbert, Jack, 58.
teachers, xiii; 20-21; 24.
teepees, Indian 40-44.
Teschemacher, Arthur, 79; 94 fn.29; 96 fn.34.
Teschemacher, Hubert E., v; vii; viii; 71; 73; 78; 79; 94-95 fn.29; 96 fn.34.
Texas, v; vii; viii; ix; x; xi; xiii; 2-31; 46; 50; ranger 51; 52-56; 67; 69; 70; 83; 84; 89 fns.2, 3; 89-90 fn.4; 90 fns.7, 8; 91 fns.10, 11; 95 fn.32; 96 fn.36.
Texas Folklore Society, 92 fn.15.
Texas Trail, vii; 90 fn.4.
"The Texas Trail," ms., x.
thieves, 2; horse 46; 61-62.
Thomason, Zacharias, 86; 88; 97 fn.39.
Thompson, Bill, 50-51.
Thompson, John Charles, xi.
Throckmorton County (Tex.), 31.
timber, 9; lack of 45; 61.
"Tobacco Jake," 58; 83.
Tom, Negro, 16; 17.
tools, trail 34.
The Trail Drivers of Texas, 91 fn.11; 93 fn.20.

trails, cattle, Northern or Texas, vii; 91 fn.9; 26; 28; 29; 31; 33; organization on, 34; Fort Worth-Ft. Dodge, 34-46; 55; Chisholm, 90 fns.6, 7; Western or Fort Griffin & Dodge City Trail, 91 fns.9, 10; crew, 91 fn.11.
Trails of Yesterday, 93 fn.19.
trees, 32; 34; 36; 37.
Trenholm, Virginia Cole, xi; 90 fn.6; 94 fn.27; 97.
Tribune, Cheyenne xi.
turkey, wild 5; 40.
turpentine, 34.

U

Uinta County, 94 fn.28.
Union Pacific Railroad, 51; 55; 69; 83; 85; 91 fn.10.
United States, Government of, 67.
University of Wyoming, x.
Utah, 93 fn.20.
Uva, 69; 78; 95 fn.32.

V

Vestal, Stanley, 92 fn.16.
Virginia, 38; 92 fn.12.
Virginia City (Mont.), 85.
volunteers, 3.

W

wages, 12; 13; negro 19; 28; 29; 34; 80; 88.
wagon, vii; ix; 9-11; 34; 37; 38; 40; 42; 48; 50; 55; 66; 67; 71; 85-88.
Walker, Robert, 79; 95 fn.32.
Ward, Bill, 55.
Warner, Howard, 26; 79; 80; 90 fn.8; 94 fn.29; 95 fn.32; 96 fn.34.
Warner, Will, 26; 79; 80; 90 fn.8; 94 fn.29; 95 fn.32; 96 fn.34.
Warren, Francis E., 52; 60; 93 fn.21; 95 fn.29.
water, vi; viii; 31; 33; 39; 43; 78;

92 fn.15.
watermelon, 46.
weather, xiii.
Webb, A. H. "Hi", 26; 90 fn.6.
Webb, Walter Prescott, vi.
West, vi; xiii; 2; 93 fn.22.
Western Range Cattle Industry Study, xi.
Western Trail, 91 fn.9.
wheelbarrow, 16.
Whipple, John M., 19.
Whipple & Hay, 95 fn.32.
whipstock, 10.
whiskey, 21-22; 29-30; 48; 51; 80-81.
Whitman, — —, 70.
Wichita (Kan.), 93 fn.20.
Wichita Hills, 39.
Williamson County (Tex.), 46.
Willis, Joe, 57; 58; 61; 63; 68.
Willow, Douglas, 79.
Winchester, rifle, 38; 46; 65.
Windy Hollow, 86.
winter, disaster 1886-1887, vi; feeding vi.
Withers, Richard, 34-50; 55; 91 fn.11.
wood[s], xiii.
"Woodbox Jim," 83.
Woodhull, Frost, 92 fn.15.
Woods, Frank, 34; 38; 39; 46; 55; 69; 92 fn.13.
work, conditions of xiii.
Wounded Knee (Dak.), 65, 67.
"wrestlers," 60.
Wyoming, vii; viii; ix; xiii; 26; 67; 78; 85; 90 fns.4, 8; 91 fn.10; 93 fns.21, 22; 94 fns.26, 28, 29; 96 fns.33, 35, 36.
Wyoming Stock Growers Association, viii; x; xi; 90 fns.4, 6; 93 fn.22; 94 fns.28, 29; 95 fns.32, 33; 96 fns.33, 34, 36; 97 fns.36-39; 97 fns.40-41.

Y

Yates, E. N., 34; 39; 45; 46; 55; 58; 60; 61; 67; 68.

1/ wymt gra

4- Boys life

13 Cattle pujns
28-23" y

49- map

52-53 Relation castle of agrden

60 an didit

74 status +75